green designed

Bianca Maria Öller

Kitchen & Dining

COOKERY . TABLEWARE . INTERIOR
KÜCHEN . GESCHIRR . INTERIEUR

avedition

01 02

Kitchen & Dining | eine Frage des guten Geschmacks.

Wer etwas auf sich hält, wer an sich, an seine Freunde und vor allem auch an seine Kinder glaubt, der kauft heute nicht mehr irgendwas ein. Bio ist das Zauberwort, wenn es darum geht, sich gesund und bewusst zu ernähren. Und was manche bereits kaufen, ohne groß darüber nachzudenken, bietet eigentlich handfeste Vorteile: Umweltbewusstsein, Respekt vor der Natur und Menschlichkeit stecken in der natürlichen Nahrung, die frei ist von künstlichen Zusatzstoffen und Geschmacksverstärkern. Nach zahlreichen Lebensmittelskandalen will man endlich wieder

wissen, woher das Stück Fleisch eigentlich kommt, das da auf dem Teller liegt. Und ob das Brot, das so lecker schmeckt, auch wirklich aus pestizidfreiem Getreide gebacken wurde. Was also beim Einkauf im Supermarkt, Reformhaus oder auf dem Wochenmarkt anfängt, hört auch zu Hause in der Küche nicht auf: Diese Speisen, die so bewusst und sorgfältig ausgesucht werden, wollen nicht irgendwo und irgendwie zubereitet werden. Nein, das Bewusstsein für Umweltfreundlichkeit, Menschenrechte, Ökosysteme und Nachhaltigkeit hat schon längst

Einzug gehalten in technische Geräte, Einrichtung und Accessoires – gerade im Küchen- und Essbereich des privaten Wohnumfelds. Nach dem Motto „das Auge und das Gewissen essen mit" schmeckt das Essen heute zu Recht gleich viel besser, wenn es in einer ökologisch korrekten Küche zubereitet und auf nachhaltigen Tellern serviert wird. Öko muss dabei natürlich längst nicht mehr „nach Öko aussehen". Namhafte Marken, renommierte Manufakturen und junge, angesagte Designer bringen Produkte auf den Markt, die in ökologisch-ökonomischer

03   04

Hinsicht überzeugen und gleichzeitig mit einem fantastischen Look glänzen: Fair Trade, Ressourcenschonung, Recycling, Nachhaltigkeit, ökologische Korrektness und vorbildliches Umweltbewusstsein treffen hier auf innovative Design-Ideen, witzige Farbkombinationen und edle Materialien. Von der Natur inspirierte Formen sowie Techniken, die Energie sparen und gleichzeitig das Leben leichter machen, lassen völlig neue Stilrichtungen entstehen, die mit altbewährten Traditionen brechen, diese weiterentwickeln und so das Design-Auge verwöhnen.

Dieses Buch stellt in drei Kapiteln – Küche, Geschirr, Interieur – Dinge vor, die nicht nur mit dem Blick auf heute, sondern vor allem auch mit dem Focus auf morgen designt wurden. Dazu zählen komplette, nachhaltige Küchensysteme, innovative, energiesparende Elektrogeräte, öko-korrekte Tische sowie Sitzgelegenheiten und jede Menge natürliche, witzige und praktische Designaccessoires, die den Alltag nicht nur schöner, sondern auch einfacher machen.

Bianca Maria Öller

01, 02 | rice, mixed tableware

03 | Ebony and Co, natural wooden floors

04 | Secto Design, octo 4240

01   02

Kitchen & Dining | a question of good taste

Those who care, those who believe in their friends and especially in their children, do not buy anything. "Organic" is the magic word when it comes to healthy and conscious food. And what some people already buy without even thinking about it, actually provides concrete benefits: environmental awareness, respect for nature and humanity are part of the natural food which is free of artificial additives and flavor enhancers. After numerous food scandals, people eventually want to know again where the piece of meets that they have on their plate, actually comes from. And if the bread which is so tasty, has really been made from pesticide-free corn. So, what starts with the shopping in the supermarket, health food shop or on the farmer's market, does not stop at home in the kitchen: these foods, which have been selected consciously and diligently, do not want to prepared anywhere, anyhow. No, the awareness for environmental friendliness, human rights, eco systems and sustainability has found its way into technical devices, appliances and accessories long ago — particularly in the kitchen and dining area of people's private living space. According to the philosophy „the eye and conscience eat first" our food rightly tastes much better today, when it has been prepared in an ecologically correct kitchen and when it is served on sustainable plates. And eco does not have to „look like eco", of course. Well-known labels, renowned manufactories and young, hip designers launch products that are convincing from the ecological-economical point of view and stand out for their stylish look at the same time: Fair Trade, resource friendliness,

03

recycling, sustainability, ecological correctness and exemplary environmental consciousness meet innovative design ideas, funny combinations of color and precious materials. Shapes and design inspired by nature and energy-saving technologies which make life easier, give rise to completely new styles that are breaking with well tried traditions, develop them and thus spoil the design eye. In three chapters—cookery, tableware, interior—this book presents things with have not only been designed with regard to the present but particularly with regard to the future. Part of it are entire, sustainable kitchen systems, innovative, energy-saving electrical appliances, ecologically correct tables and seats as well as plenty of natural, funny and practical design accessories which make everyday life not only more beautiful but also a lot easier.

Bianca Maria Öller

01 | Loft and Lounge, sit down, sit & eat

02 | Tom Dixon, Slab

03 | Nils Holger Moormann, Erika

Data and Facts		Instant Kitchen
Material	Material	FSC-certified wood | FSC zertifiziertes Holz
Sustainability	Nachhaltigkeit	durability, flexibility | Beständigkeit, Flexibilität
Manufacture	Verarbeitung	natural oils, water-based adhesive | natürliche Öle, wasserbasierter Leim
Fair Trade	Fair Trade	made in Denmark | made in Denmark

Instant Kitchen | Hansen Living

www.hansenliving.com

The Danish wood manufactory Hansen Living produces outstanding minimalistic furniture designed by executive designer Knud Kapper. Apart from the requirement to convince with innovative design, Hansen Living sets value on exclusively producing eco-friendly and sustainable furniture from the very beginning. The company therefore uses materials that develop a natural patina in the course of the years and the older they get—and thus become more and more beautiful. Just like wood originating from FSC-certified woods which are processed and finished with water-based glues and natural oils. Unique pieces of furniture such as the Instant Kitchen are the result of this skillful design and sophisticated way of production. A puristic kitchen unit made of stainless steel and wood can be installed anywhere according to the motto „just add water" and finds its place in every new home over and over again in times of mobility. Equipped with oven, refrigerator and sink, the Instant Kitchen is ready for use anytime, anywhere.

Die dänische Holzmanufaktur Hansen Living bringt unter der kreativen Leitung von Chefdesigner Knud Kapper herausragendes, minimalistisches Design hervor. Neben dem Anspruch, mit innovativer Gestaltung zu überzeugen, hat Hansen Living von Beginn an Wert darauf gelegt, nur umweltfreundliche und nachhaltige Möbel zu schaffen. Sie verwenden deshalb Materialien, die mit den Jahren und mit dem Gebrauch eine natürliche Patina entwickeln. Und so immer schöner werden. Wie Hölzer aus FSC zertifizierten Wäldern, die mit wasserbasierten Leimen und natürlichen Ölen bearbeitet und veredelt werden. Das Ergebnis dieses gekonnten Designs und durchdachten Produktionsweges sind so einzigartige Stücke wie die Instant Kitchen. Ein puristischer Küchenblock aus Edelstahl und Holz, der nach dem Motto „just add water" überall aufgebaut werden kann. Der in einer Zeit der Mobilität in jedem neuen Zuhause wieder seinen Platz findet. Und mit Gasherd, Backofen, Kühlschrank und Spüle immer und überall sofort einsatzbereit ist.

Data and Facts		Refrigerator
Energy efficiency | Energieeffizienz		A++ | A++
Technology | Technologie		innovative BioFresh technology | innovative BioFresh Technologie
Design | Design		PlusX, red dot Award | PlusX, Red Dot Award

Cooling units | Liebherr

www.liebherr.de

A refrigerator is an absolute must-have in every kitchen. And hardly any household can do without a freezer. And lovers of wine also rely on an electric appliance for storing wines: the wine storage cabinet. Liebherr proves that these appliances can be extremely energy-saving and therefore eco-friendly and even look pretty good at the same time. As a result, the built-in refrigerator IKB 3453 with BioFresh technology has been honored with the PlusXAward for ease of use and ecology in 2007. The table-height freezer GP 1466 with SmartFrost complies with the exceptional energy efficiency class A++. The wine storage cabinet WTes 4677 took even two design awards: the PlusXAward Design in 2007 and the red dot Award in 2008. And the integrated built-in refrigerator-freezer combination ICBN 3066 has been elected kitchen innovation of the year by the initiative „Besser Leben". However, Liebherr does not lay back with those awards in their shelves. In autumn 2008, Liebherr launches the world's most energy-saving freezer of its size. And the designers constantly keep developing new, likely to win an award and functional cooling and freezing appliances.

Ein Kühlschrank ist ein absolutes Muss in jeder Küche. Auch ohne einen Gefrierschrank kommt kaum ein Haushalt aus. Und Genießer setzen auch bei der Lagerung von Wein auf ein Elektrogerät: den Weinklimaschrank. Dass diese Geräte äußerst energiesparend und damit umweltverträglich sein können und gleichzeitig auch noch richtig gut aussehen können, zeigt die Marke Liebherr. So wurde der Einbaukühlschrank IKB 3453 mit BioFresh-Technologie im Jahr 2007 mit dem PlusXAward für Bedienkomfort und Ökologie ausgezeichnet. Der Tischgefrierschrank GPes 1466 mit SmartFrost erfüllt die herausragende Energieeffizienzklasse A++. Der Weintemperierschrank WTes 4677 heimste gleich zwei Designpreise ein: den PlusXAward Design 2007 und den red dot Award 2008. Und die Einbau-Kühl-Gefrierkombination ICBN 3066 wurde 2007 von der Initiative „Besser Leben" zur Kücheninnovation des Jahres gekürt. Auf diesen Erfolgen ruht sich Liebherr nicht aus. Im Herbst 2008 kommt die weltweit energiesparendste Gefriertruhe ihrer Literklasse auf den Markt. Und die Designer entwickeln neue, preisverdächtig gestaltete und funktionale Kühl- und Gefriergeräte

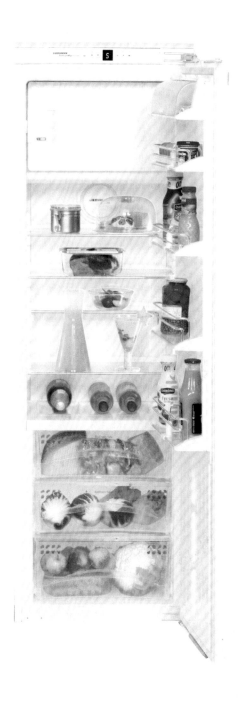

Data and Facts		Sommelier Series	
Material	Material	Engl Text starts here	gebürsteter, rostfreier Edelstahl	
Sustainability	Nachhaltigkeit	Engl Text starts here	Beständigkeit, recyclingfähiges Material	
Technology	Technologie	Engl Text starts here	energiesparendes Expresskochsystem (Wasserkocher), integrierter Brita Wasserfilter und Abschaltautomatik (Kaffeemaschine)	

Sommelier Series | Braun

www.braun.com

According to the philosophy „Design your life", Braun launches a kitchen line of electrical appliances which stand for aesthetic and quality right down into the last detail and set new standards with their innovative, functional and resource-friendly technologies as well as the high-quality, fantastic processing for which Braun is known. The Sommelier series consists of a kettle, a coffee machine and a toaster – the typical appliances which may not be missing in any kitchen. Those little kitchen utensils do not only look stylish thanks to their swinging lines and the cool brushed stainless steel but also provide for sustainable technology: the Sommelier water kettle therefore takes only 45 seconds to boil 200 ml of water due to its innovative express boiling system. This saves energy—just like the practical shut off automatic of the coffee maker which provides for the machine to be shut off automatically as soon as coffee is ready. Instead of an energy-consuming hot plate for keeping coffee hot, Braun uses a stylishly designed vacuum insulated carafe. And thanks to the integrated Brita water filter, the coffee is not only particularly tasty—the coffee maker also works exceptionally efficient as it hardly calcifies.

Unter dem Motto „Design your life" bringt die Marke Braun Elektrogeräte für die Küche auf den Markt, die für Ästhetik und Qualität bis ins kleinste Detail stehen. Und mit ihren innovativen, funktionalen und ressourcenschonenden Technologien sowie der hochwertigen, eine für Braun charakteristische Verarbeitung, neue Maßstäbe setzen. Die Serie Sommelier besteht aus einem Wasserkocher, einer Kaffeemaschine und einem Toaster – den typischen Kleingeräten, die in keiner Küche fehlen dürfen. Diese sehen mit ihren schwungvollen Linien und dem coolen, gebürsteten Edelstahl nicht nur sehr hochwertig aus. Die kleinen Helfer bringen auch nachhaltige Technik mit: So bringt der Sommelier Wasserkocher mit seinem neuartigen Expresskochsystem 200ml Wasser in nur 45 Sekunden zum Sieden. Das spart Energie – genau wie die praktische Abschaltautomatik, die bei der Kaffeemaschine dafür sorgt, dass diese sich ausschaltet, sobald der Kaffee fertig ist. Anstatt einer stromfressenden Warmhalteplatte setzt Braun hier auf eine Isolierkanne in edlem Design. Und dank des integrierten Brita Wasserfilters schmeckt der Kaffee nicht nur besonders lecker – die Kaffeemaschine arbeitet auch außergewöhnlich effizient, da sie kaum verkalkt.

Data and Facts	Primus LED Light
Material	Verarbeitung	eco-friendly CRISTALITE®	umweltfreundliches CRISTALITE®
Sustainability	Nachhaltigkeit	durability, longevity	Beständigkeit, Langlebigkeit
Technology	Technologie	economical LED lighting	sparsame LED-Beleuchtung
Fair Trade	Fair Trade	made in Germany	made in Germany

LED Sink | Schock

www.schock.de

Real highlights in every kitchen are the design sinks of Schock, innovatively lighted with LED lights that are as attractive as functional. The Primus sink is made of the highly modern composite material CRISTALITE®—a high quality composite material which is eco-friendly at the same time. This waterproof, light- and colorfast material is predominantly made of natural raw materials as well as of recycling material. In further processing Schock pays special attention to the fact that energy input is low. And built-in into your kitchen at home, the sink's robust surface stands out for a high durability and sustainability. The innovative LED lighting helps to save energy: LEDs are extremely economical, have a long service life and still provide for high performance. Installation directly in the sink guarantees for well directed lightness exactly where it is needed. It is therefore not necessary to light the entire kitchen after a small midnight snack, for instance, just to clean a glass. The LEDs are controlled via a handy function switch.

Ein echtes Highlight in der Küche sind die Designspülen von Schock, innovativ beleuchtet mit ebenso attraktiven wie funktionalen LED-Leuchten. Die Spüle Primus wird aus dem hochmodernen Composite-Werkstoff CRISTALITE® hergestellt – ein Material höchster Güte, das zugleich die Umwelt schont. Der wasserfeste, licht- und farbechte Werkstoff wird aus überwiegend natürlichen Rohstoffen sowie aus Recycling-Material hergestellt. In der Weiterverarbeitung wird bei Schock auf einen reduzierten Energieaufwand geachtet. Und eingebaut in der heimischen Küche steht die robuste Oberfläche der Spüle für eine hohe Langlebigkeit und Nachhaltigkeit. Die innovative LED-Beleuchtung hilft zudem beim Energiesparen: LEDs sind äußerst sparsam und haben eine lange Lebensdauer, trotzdem sind sie sehr leistungsstark. Der Einbau direkt im Becken sorgt für gezielte Helligkeit genau dort wo sie gebraucht wird. So muss z.B. nach einem kleinen Mitternachtssnack nicht mehr die ganze Küche beleuchtet werden, nur um ein Glas abzuspülen. Bedient werden die LED über einen praktischen Funkschalter.

Data and Facts		Wattson
Ecology | Umweltschutz		support in energy-saving | Unterstützung beim Energiesparen
Technology | Technologie		state-of-the-art, low-radiation radio technology | moderne, strahlungsarme Funktechnologie
Fair Trade | Fair Trade		made in the United Kingdom | made in United Kingdom

Wattson | Diy Kyoto

www.diykyoto.com

Stove, oven, refrigerator, coffee machine... the list of energy-consuming devices in the kitchen seems to be endless. However, which appliance does actually use how much of the valuable energy—and where are unexpected saving potentials? The energy measuring device Wattson provides the answers to these questions—and looks quite stylish by the way. Wattson allocates all electrical appliances in its environment via radio technology and measures their consumption. This will then—already transferred into a € or £ price—be displayed on the front side of the device in red digits. As an orientation aid, Wattson also changes its lighting on the down side: the bluer the light, the lower the energy consumption. The redder it gets, the more energy is consumed by the handy kitchen appliances. Wattson is able to evaluate all measurements on the PC by means of a computer program. In doing so, not only the energy consumption will be indicated but also the saving potentials and possibilities to generate power.

Herd, Backofen, Kühlschrank, Kaffeemaschine, ... die Liste der Stromfresser in der Küche scheint schier endlos zu sein. Doch welches Gerät verbraucht eigentlich wie viel von der wertvollen Energie – und wo steckt ungeahntes Sparpotenzial? Das Energiemessgerät Wattson gibt darauf Antwort. Und sieht zudem auch noch richtig stylish aus. Per Funktechnologie ortet Wattson alle elektrischen Geräte in seiner Umgebung und misst deren Verbrauch. Dieser wird dann – bereits umgerechnet in eine Kostenangabe in € oder £ – auf der Oberseite des Geräts in rot leuchtenden Zahlen angezeigt. Als Orientierungshilfe ändert Wattson zudem seine Beleuchtung auf der Unterseite: Je blauer das Licht, desto geringer ist der Stromverbrauch. Wird es rötlicher, fließt umso mehr Energie durch die praktischen Küchengeräte. Mittels eines Computerprogramms lassen sich die Messungen von Wattson am PC auswerten. Dabei wird nicht nur der Energieverbrauch aufgezeigt, sondern auch Einsparpotenziale und Möglichkeiten um Energie zu erzeugen.

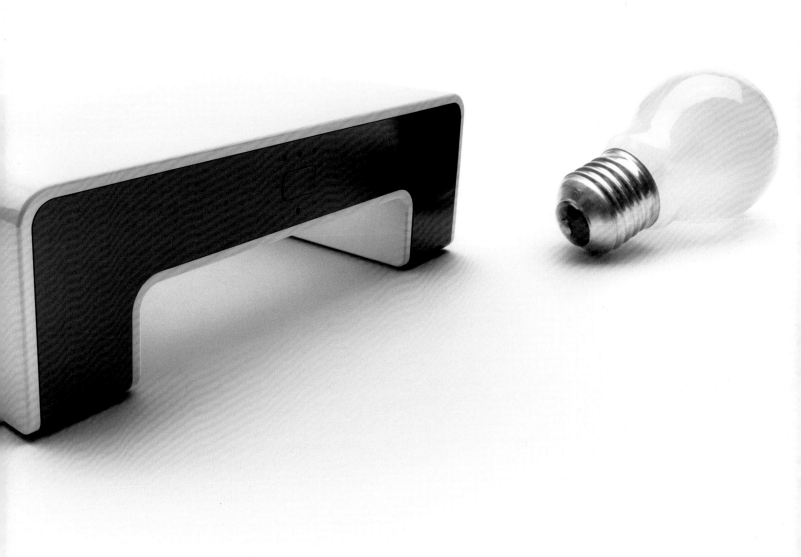

Data and Facts		Faktum
Ecology | Umweltschutz		recycling/waste disposal, economical use of energy | Recycling/Müllentsorgung, sparsamer Umgang mit Energie
Sustainability | Nachhaltigkeit		wood originating from ecological forestry | Holz aus ökologischer Forstwirtschaft
Fair Trade | Fair Trade		cotton from Fair Trade cultivation | Baumwolle aus Fair Trade Anbau
Social commitment | Soziales Engagement		co-operations with WWF, Unicef, Save the Children | Kooperationen mit WWF, Unicef, Save the Children

Kitchen system Faktum | IKEA

www.ikea.com

For those who are concerned about an ecologically correct and environmental furnishing concept, IKEA will probably not be the first on the list. IKEA is a company that sets standards all over the world when it comes to economical and ecological exemplary acting, though. Thus, every IKEA branch has an Environmental Coordinator who is responsible for business waste disposal and energy efficiency. Using wood from responsibly farmed forests as well as fair and environmentally sound cultivated cotton completes the range of resource-friendly timeless furniture ideas that therefore also stand for longevity and a high level of sustainability. Along with this comes the high social responsibility IKEA accepts in co-operations with WWF, Unicef and Save the Children. The result of that much social and ecological commitment is furniture which providing fun and convince with fresh Scandinavian design. A good example for this is the Faktum kitchen system which brings life into the kitchen which brings life to the kitchen with fresh Scandinavian design which can be adapted to one's individual lifestyle due to a variety of different fronts.

Wer sich Gedanken macht über ein ökologisch korrektes und umweltbewusstes Einrichtungskonzept, wird nicht unbedingt IKEA an erster Stelle auf seiner Liste haben. Dabei ist IKEA ein Unternehmen, das weltweit Maßstäbe setzt, wenn es um ökonomisch und ökologisch vorbildliches Handeln geht. So hat jeder IKEA Standort einen Umweltkoordinator, der für Müllentsorgung und Energieeffizienz zuständig ist. Holz aus verantwortungsvoll bewirtschafteten Wäldern sowie fair und umweltschonend angebaute Baumwolle komplettieren ressourcenschonende, zeitlose Möbelideen, die damit auch für Langlebigkeit und eine hohe Nachhaltigkeit stehen. Hinzu kommt die hohe gesellschaftliche Verantwortung, die IKEA in Kooperationen mit WWF, Unicef und Save the Children übernimmt. Heraus kommen bei soviel sozialem und ökologischem Engagement Einrichtungsgegenstände, die Spaß machen und mit frischem skandinavischen Design überzeugen. Wie das Faktum Küchensystem, das Leben in die Küche bringt. Und durch eine Vielzahl abwechslungsreicher Fronten an das individuelle Lebensgefühl angepasst werden kann.

Data and Facts	Nespresso
Technology | Technologie	coffee machines with state-of-the-art, energy-efficient standards | Kaffeemaschinen mit modernen, energieeffizienten Standards
Sustainability | Nachhaltigkeit	improved relationship between consumer and coffee farmer | Verbesserung der Beziehung von Konsument und Kaffeebauer
Fair Trade | Fair Trade	coffee from Fair Trade cultivation | Kaffee aus nachhaltigem Kaffeeanbau

Le Cube & Lattissima | Nespresso

www.nespresso.com

The Nespresso coffee system is based on aroma capsules filled with coffee and on coffee machines for different demands, which are filled with the aforementioned capsules. When developing new coffee machines in cooperation with partners such as Krups or De'Longhi, Nespresso always aims to set new design trends and to come up with the requirements of the up-market furnishing standard. The trendy little cube "Le cube" and the stylish multi-talent "Lattissima" are successful examples for this statement. And the little coffee capsules also set an optical course—however, apart from their unique appearance, its content plays the much more important role: the coffee. And this is exactly where Nespresso walks an exemplary way of sustainability with its company-own program "AAA Sustainable Quality": with coffee complying with highest quality standards, a fair salary system for farmers in the producing countries and pursuing the goal to bring end consumers and farmers closer together in order to achieve more mutual understanding and long-term respect.

Das Nespresso Kaffeesystem beruht auf Aromakapseln, die mit Kaffee gefüllt sind. Und auf Kaffeemaschinen für unterschiedlichste Ansprüche, die mit diesen Kapseln befüllt werden. Bei der Entwicklung neuer Geräte legt Nespresso gemeinsam mit Kooperationspartnern wie Krups oder De'Longhi stets Wert darauf, neue Designtrends zu setzen und den Ansprüchen an gehobene Einrichtungsstandards gerecht zu werden. Der hippe, kleine Würfel „Le Cube" und das stylishe Multitalent „Lattissima" sind dafür gelungene Beispiele. Auch die kleinen Kaffeekapseln setzen optische Akzente – doch neben ihrem einzigartigen Äußeren spielt hier der Inhalt eine viel wichtigere Rolle: der Kaffee. Und bei genau diesem geht Nespresso mit dem firmeneigenen Programm „AAA Sustainable Quality" einen vorbildlichen Weg der Nachhaltigkeit: mit Kaffee, der höchsten Qualitätsstandards entspricht, mit einem fairen Lohnsystem für die Kaffeebauern in den Anbauländern und mit dem Ziel, die Endverbraucher und die Kaffeebauern näher zusammenzubringen, um mehr gegenseitiges Verständnis und langfristigen Respekt zu erreichen.

Data and Facts		Lacquerware & Nesting Baskets
Material	Material	ecologically correct bamboo | ökologisch korrekter Bambus
Sustainability	Nachhaltigkeit	fast re-growing raw material | schnell nachwachsender Rohstoff
Manufacture	Verarbeitung	eco-friendly colors and adhesives | umweltverträgliche Farben und Klebstoffe
Fair Trade	Fair Trade	Member of Co-op America | Mitglied von Co-op America

Lacquerware & Nesting Baskets | Bambu

www.bambuhome.com

Bamboo is a renewable, fast re-growing material which is ecologically cultivated, processed in various ways and which can even be eaten. So what suggests itself more than to create sustainable, stylish kitchen accessories made of bamboo? According to this principle, Bambu designs innovative and attractive products for kitchen and dining table—such as friendly colored Lacquerware bowls or the lightweight Nesting Baskets. These are made from organically grown bamboo and exclusively finished with environmentally friendly, water-based adhesives and lacquers. All of the production facilities are in China and Vietnam and all manufacturing partners have to meet Bambu's Fair Trade principles for acceptable labor practices and conditions. Bambu moreover is a member of the Co-op American Business Network. Bambu employees regularly visit the villages and production sites to convince themselves that the stylish bamboo utensils are manufactured according to fair and ecologically acceptable conditions.

Bambus ist ein erneuerbares Material, das schnell nachwächst, dabei ökologisch angebaut, vielfältig verarbeitet und sogar gegessen werden kann. Was liegt also näher, als nachhaltige, stylishe Küchenhelfer aus Bambus zu schaffen? Nach diesem Prinzip designt Bambu innovative und attraktive Produkte für Küche und Esstisch – wie die fröhlich-bunten Lacquerware Schüsseln oder die leichten Nesting Baskets. Diese werden aus organisch gewachsenem Bio-Bambus produziert und ausschließlich mit umweltverträglichen, wasserbasierten Klebstoffen sowie Lacken behandelt. Alle Produktionsstätten liegen dabei in China und Vietnam und müssen sich dazu verpflichten Fair Trade Aspekte wie menschliche Arbeitsbedingungen und Löhne einzuhalten. Bambu kooperiert dazu mit der Aktion „Co-op American Business Network". Außerdem bereisen Mitarbeiter von Bambu regelmäßig die Produktionsstätten, um sich selbst davon zu überzeugen, dass die stylishen Bambusutensilien unter fairen und ökologisch einwandfreien Bedingungen hergestellt werden.

Data and Facts		Mikoto
Material | Material		ecologically correct bamboo | ökologisch korrekter Bambus
Sustainability | Nachhaltigkeit		fast re-growing raw material | schnell nachwachsender Rohstoff
Manufacture | Verarbeitung		eco-friendly finishes | umweltverträgliche Lacke
Fair Trade | Fair Trade		fair production in Vietnam | faire Produktion in Vietnam

Mikoto | Ekobo
www.ekobo.org

Ekobo combines timeless and at the same time contemporary design with fruity-tasty colors and a work ethic which is just as thoughtful as ethically correct. All these exceptional kitchen accessories of the young French designer are therefore handcrafted in Vietnamese villages under best Fair Trade conditions. Artisans are realizing visionary products such as the knife block Mikoto by using traditional working methods and ecologically correct materials. Mikoto is therefore made of fast re-growing bamboo which exclusively originates from controlled cultivation. Only environmentally paints are used for the finishing in terms of colors. Craftsmen can stay in their villages to do their work in small local workshops—an important part of Ekobo's concept as an ongoing urbanization and formation of slums can only be avoided on the long term by creating more jobs in the rural areas of developing countries. This is meaningful—and particularly great when unique pieces of design such as the Mikoto knife block are created at the same time.

Ekobo kombiniert zeitloses und zugleich zeitgemäßes Design mit fruchtig-leckeren Farben und einer ebenso bedachten wie ethisch-korrekten Arbeitsmoral. So werden die außergewöhnlichen Küchenhelfer der französischen Jungdesigner in vietnamesischen Dörfern unter besten Fair Trade Bedingungen hergestellt. Handwerker realisieren dort visionäre Produkte, wie den Messerblock Mikoto, mit traditionellen Arbeitsmethoden und ökologisch korrekten Materialien. So wird Mikoto aus schnell nachwachsendem Bambus produziert, der ausschließlich aus kontrolliertem Anbau stammt. Und die farbliche Veredelung erfolgt nur mit umweltverträglichen Lacken. Die Handwerker können dabei in ihren Dörfern bleiben und ihre Arbeit in den kleinen heimischen Werkstätten ausführen – ein wichtiger Teil des Konzepts von Ekobo: Denn nur durch die Schaffung von Arbeitsplätzen in den ländlichen Gegenden der Entwicklungsländer kann langfristig eine weitere Urbanisierung und Slumbildung vermieden werden. Dies ist sinnvoll – und besonders schön, wenn dabei auch noch so einzigartige Designstücke wie der Mikoto Messerblock entstehen.

Data and Facts	KG28FM50
Energy efficiency | Energieeffizienz	A+ | A+
Technology | Technologie	vitaFresh, defrost-automatic, 17"-LCD-Display | vitaFresh, Abtau-Automatik, 17"-LCD-Fernseher
Design | Design	Unobtrusive in high-quality stainless steel | zurückhaltend in schwarz, überstehende Glastüren

KG28FM50 | Siemens

www.siemens-homeappliances.com, www.siemens-hausgeraete.de

The household appliances of Siemens stand for best quality. And the rich-in-tradition company also sets standards when it comes to sustainability, ecology and energy efficiency: the current home appliances of Siemens work so economically that they do with a minimum of power and water. However, at the same time, the appliances did not suffer in terms of comfort and design. Far from it! KG28FM50 shows that an innovative 3-in-1 cooling appliance, cooling, fresh-cooling and freezing, can look high-quality. Additionally the 17"-LCD-Display makes sure to have good entertainment. And with energy efficiency class A+, it also does good for ecology. Moreover, with eco star, Siemens supplies a line which stands out for enormously low energy consumption: freezer GS40NA35, for instance, which even exceeds the A++ requirements and still fulfills all functions of a demanding freezer such as the noFrost technology, thanks to which laborious "manual" defrosting is a thing of the past. Developers of Siemens are constantly working to further reduce consumption values in order to relieve climate and household budget in the future as well. The only point in which refrigerators and freezers are lavish then, is comfort.

Die Hausgeräte von Siemens stehen für höchste Qualität. Und auch wenn es um Nachhaltigkeit, Umweltschutz und Energieeffizienz geht, setzt das Traditionsunternehmen Maßstäbe: Die aktuellen Hausgeräte von Siemens arbeiten so ökonomisch, dass sie ein Minimum an Strom und Wasser verbrauchen. Gleichzeitig haben die Geräte aber nichts an Komfort und Design eingebüßt. Im Gegenteil: die neue Kühl-Gefrier-Kombination KG28FM50 beweist, dass ein innovatives 3-in-1-Kältegerät, das Kühlen, Frischkühlen und Gefrieren vereint, sehr hochwertig aussehen kann, dabei mit einem 17"-LCD-Display für Unterhaltung sorgt, und zugleich mit der Energieeffizienzklasse A+ auch in ökologischer Hinsicht überzeugt. Des Weiteren vertreibt Siemens unter dem Namen eco star eine Linie, die mit einer enormen Sparsamkeit beim Energieverbrauch glänzt: Zum Beispiel der Gefrierschrank GS40NA35, der die A++ Anforderungen sogar noch übertrifft und dabei alle Funktionen eines anspruchsvollen Gefriergerätes besitzt. Wie die noFrost-Technologie, mit der mühsames Abtauen „von Hand" der Vergangenheit angehört. Damit Klima und Haushaltskasse auch in Zukunft entlastet werden, arbeiten Siemens-Entwickler laufend daran, die Verbrauchswerte weiter zu senken. Verschwenderisch sind Kühl- und Gefriergeräte dann nur noch in dem Punkt Komfort.

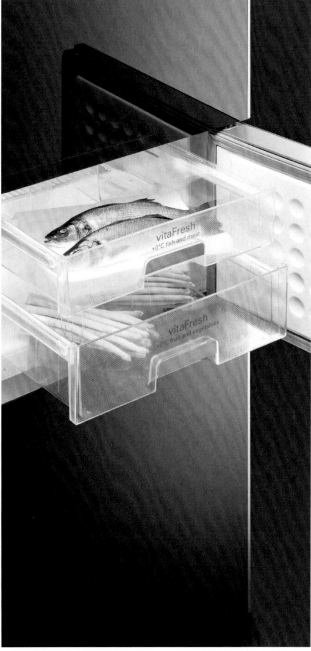

Data and Facts		Enamel pots	
Material	Material	natural raw materials	natürliche Rohstoffe
Sustainability	Nachhaltigkeit	durability, longevity	Beständigkeit, Langlebigkeit
Evidence of suitability	Entsorgbarkeit	completely recyclable	komplett recyclebar
Fair Trade	Fair Trade	made in Austria	made in Austria

Enamel pots | Grüne Erde

www.grueneerde.com

Enamel tableware is manufactured from natural raw materials such as steel, quartz, feldspath, borax, soda and potash. In everyday use it is exceptionally resistant, light- and colorfast, anti-bacterial and hygienic, which makes it an extremely durable and popular household material. Should it really be disposed at some stage, enamel tableware is completely recyclable. All enamel products "Grüne Erde" supplies originate from the rich in tradition enamel works Riess in Lower Austria. The tableware is manufactured in compliance with highest ecological standards. The designs are inspired by traditional and partially century old Austrian classics such as the simple bread box to hygienically store bread and small pastries, the small and handy egg pan or the pretty kitchen tools which do not have to hide in the drawer. With their unobtrusive designs and the timeless white enamel, the individual pieces perfectly fit harmoniously in both puristic-modern kitchen concepts and an attention to detail country-house kitchen.

Emailgeschirr wird aus den natürlichen Rohstoffen Stahl, Quarz, Feldspat, Borax, Soda und Pottasche hergestellt. Im täglichen Gebrauch ist es außergewöhnlich widerstandsfähig, lichtecht, farbbeständig, antibakteriell und hygienisch, was es zu einem extrem langlebigen und seit jeher beliebten Haushaltsmaterial macht. Wird es doch einmal entsorgt, ist Emailgeschirr vollständig recyclingfähig. Die Emailprodukte, die Grüne Erde vertreibt, kommen aus den traditionsreichen Emaillierwerken Riess in Niederösterreich. Das Geschirr wird dort unter Einhaltung höchster ökologischer Standards produziert. Die Formendesigns greifen althergebrachte und zum Teil jahrhundertealte österreichische Klassiker auf. Wie die schlichte Brotdose zum hygienischen Aufbewahren von Brot und Kleingebäck, die handliche kleine Eierpfanne oder auch die schmucken Küchenwerkzeuge, die sich in keiner Schublade zu verstecken brauchen. Mit ihren dezenten Formen und dem zeitlosen weißen Email fügen sich die einzelnen Stücke in ein puristisch-modernes Küchenkonzept ebenso harmonisch ein wie in eine detailverliebte Landhausküche.

Data and Facts		Recycler
Material | Material		stainless steel, plastics | Edelstahl, Kunststoff
Sustainability | Nachhaltigkeit		durable processing, classic design | langlebige Verarbeitung, klassisches Design
Fair Trade | Fair Trade		made in the United States | made in United States

Recycler | Simplehuman

www.simplehuman.com

Ecological correct waste disposal and a furnishing concept with the highest demands to design do not go together? Simplehuman answers this question with a clear "no". The company's waste systems both focus on functional and elegant designs, realized in timeless brushed stainless steel. Therefore, the puristically designed recycler takes up his place in the kitchen just as a matter of course without attracting too much attention. And the trash can makes a good job of it: two separate waste containers take up 19 liters of residual waste and recyclable waste each. Tightly closed by a cover which can be operated by a foot pedal, it avoids unpleasant smells and looks always dazzling thanks to the innovative fingerprint-proof technology: smudges from wastes or hands do not stick to the nice stainless steel surface at all. This contemporary system is complemented by accessories such as a corresponding bag dispenser. Waste separation becomes so easy and chic – it is therefore no wonder that the innovative system is regularly honored with international design awards.

Ökologisch korrekte Mülltrennung und ein Einrichtungskonzept mit höchstem Designanspruch passen nicht zusammen? Simplehuman beantwortet diese Frage mit einem klaren „Nein". Ihre Abfallsysteme setzen auf ebenso funktionale wie elegante Formen, realisiert in zeitlosem gebürsteten Edelstahl. So nimmt der puristisch designte Recycler in der Küche wie selbstverständlich seinen Platz ein, ohne groß aufzufallen. Und leistet dabei ganze Arbeit: Zwei voneinander getrennte Müllbehälter schlucken je 19 Liter Restmüll und wiederverwertbare Abfälle. Dicht verschlossen von einer per Fußpedal bedienbaren Abdeckung verhindert er die Entstehung unangenehmer Gerüche. Und sieht dabei dank innovativer finger-print-proof Technologie stets blendend aus: Schmierflecken von Abfällen oder den Händen bleiben damit an der edlen Edelstahloberfläche erst gar nicht haften. Komplettiert wird das zeitgemäße System von Zubehör wie einem passenden Tütenspender. Mülltrennen wird so einfach und chic – kein Wunder also, dass das innovative System regelmäßig mit internationalen Designpreisen ausgezeichnet wird.

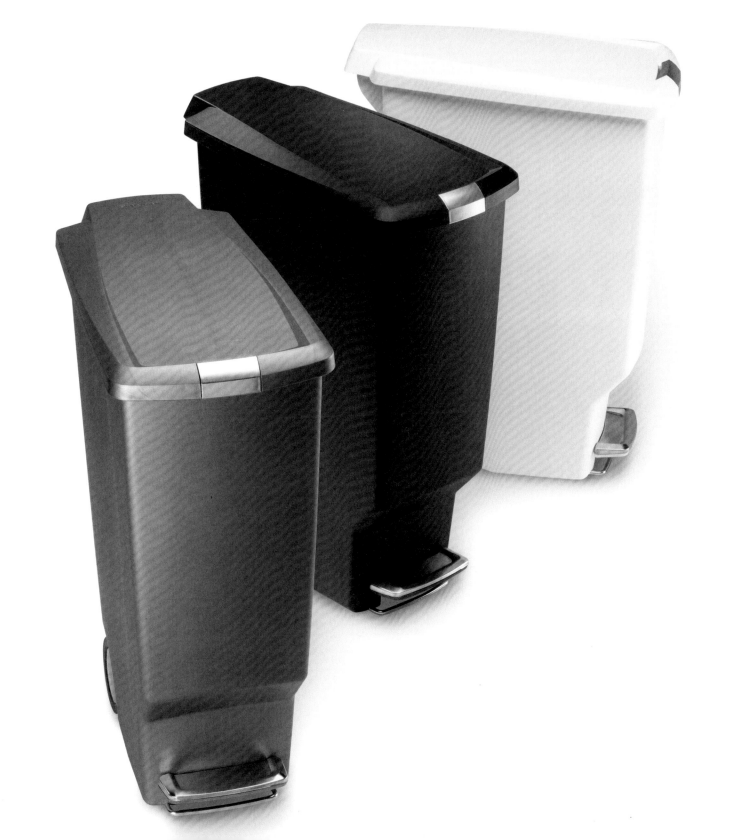

Data and Facts		Kitchen k7
Material	Material	local hardwood, glass, stainless steel | heimische Laubhölzer, Glas, Edelstahl
Manufacture	Verarbeitung	natural oils, water-based adhesives | natürliche Öle, wasserbasierte Leime
Sustainability	Nachhaltigkeit	durable processing, classic design | langlebige Verarbeitung, klassisches Design
Technology	Technologie	innovative, height-adjustable worktop, Servo-Drive | innovative, höhenverstellbare Arbeitsplatte, Servo-Drive
Fair Trade	Fair Trade	made in Austria | made in Austria

Kitchen k7 | TEAM 7

www.team7.at

Design meets nature—this is the slogan of the internationally renowned premium brand TEAM 7 from Austria. And kitchen k7 exactly lives this mission statement. Its massive wood corpuses comply with highest ecological standards both when it comes to the choice of local hardwood and its processing with natural oils as well as water-based glues. And the combination with high-quality stainless steel and glass, the integration of innovative technology and the open room concept make k7 an absolutely unique design object. The height-adjustable work top of the stand-alone kitchen unit underlines the unique versatility and inimitable high sustainability of this kitchen—does it work as a work top, dining table and counter top at the same time. The fronts without handles are also immediately striking the eye. Thanks to Servo-Drive, drawers can be easily opened just by tipping it with hand, knee or feet. There's even more technology hidden in the sink: due to foldaway fittings the sink can be completely covered and be therefore used as an expanded work or counter top.

Design trifft Natur – so lautet das Motto der internationalen Premium-Marke TEAM 7 aus Österreich. Und genau diesen Leitspruch lebt die Küche k7. Ihre Massivholzkorpusse entsprechen höchsten ökologischen Standards, bei der Wahl der heimischen Laubhölzer ebenso wie in der Verarbeitung mit natürlichen Ölen sowie wasserbasierten Leimen. Und die Kombination mit hochwertigem Edelstahl und Glas, die Integration innovativer Technik sowie das offene Raumkonzept machen k7 zu einem einzigartigen Designobjekt. Die höhenverstellbare Arbeitsplatte des frei-stehenden Küchenblocks unterstreicht dabei die einzigartige Vielseitigkeit und unnachahmlich hohe Nachhaltigkeit der Küche – fungiert sie doch gleichzeitig als Arbeitsplatte, Esstisch und Bartresen. Augenfällig werden auch sofort die grifflosen Fronten. Sie lassen sich per Servo-Drive ganz einfach durch Antippen mit den Händen oder auch mit dem Knie oder den Füßen öffnen. Weitere Technik ist im Spülbecken versteckt: Durch versenkbare Armaturen kann das Spülbecken vollständig abgedeckt und so als erweiterte Arbeitsfläche oder Barbereich genutzt werden.

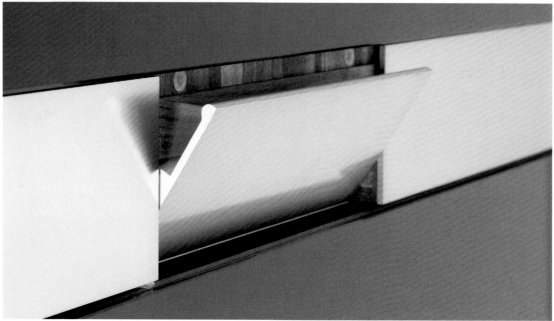

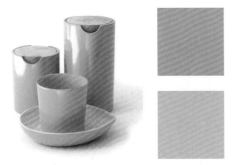

Data and Facts		Globo, Plato, ...
Material	Material	ecological correct bamboo | ökologisch korrekter Bambus
Sustainability	Nachhaltigkeit	fast re-growing raw material | schnell nachwachsender Rohstoff
Manufacture	Verarbeitung	eco-friendly finishes | umweltverträgliche Lacke
Fair Trade	Fair Trade	fair production in Vietnam | faire Produktion in Vietnam

Medio, Gemo | Ekobo

www.ekobo.org

One can never have enough beautiful bowls, big and small trays and various plates in a kitchen. Ekobo's product range of kitchen equipment offers a wide choice here—ecologically correct made of environmentally friendly cultivated, fast growing bamboo. The multi-national designers of the ekobo team play with plenty of fresh, fruity colors. The contrast between the brightly painted outsides and the natural, creatively grained bamboo on the insides makes the kitchen equipment striking and exceptional. The most various innovative forms are geared to gentle curves, natural undulations and the beauty of simple, functional openings. Those fashionable little accessories are all hand-crafted in Vietnamese villages. Creative local craftsmen are working there for ekobo under Fair Trade conditions: they receive a salary that is approximately two times higher than what the average population receives and ekobo pays its artisans directly instead of having middlemen.

Schöne Schüsseln, kleine und große Tabletts sowie unterschiedliche Teller kann man in einer Küche nie genug haben. Die Produktpalette an Küchenutensilien von ekobo bietet da eine breitgefächerte Auswahl – ökologisch korrekt aus umweltgerecht angebautem, schnell nachwachsendem Bambus. Das multinationale Designerteam von ekobo spielt dabei mit einer Fülle an frischen, fruchtigen Farbtönen. Der Kontrast zwischen den glänzend lackierten Außenseiten und dem naturbelassenen, kreativ gemaserten Bambus der Innenseiten macht die Küchenutensilien auffällig und ungewöhnlich. Und verschiedenste innovative Formen orientieren sich an sanften Rundungen, natürlichen Wellenbewegungen sowie an der Schönheit einfacher, funktionaler Aussparungen. Hergestellt werden die kleinen Helfer in vietnamesischen Dörfern. Kreative Handwerker arbeiten dort unter Fair Trade Bedingungen für ekobo: Sie erhalten etwa doppelt soviel Lohn wie die durchschnittliche Bevölkerung und dieser wird hier anstatt über Mittelsmänner von ekobo direkt an sie ausbezahlt.

Data and Facts	Kitchen Jovanella
Material | Material	beech/oak solid wood, glass, stainless steel | Buchen-/Eichenvollholz, Glas, Edelstahl
Manufacture | Verarbeitung	natural oils | natürliche Öle
Sustainability | Nachhaltigkeit	durable processing, classy design | langlebige Verarbeitung, zurückhaltendes Design
Technology | Technologie	energy-saving electrical appliances | energiesparende Elektrogeräte
Fair Trade | Fair Trade	made in Austria | made in Austria

Kitchen Jovanella | Grüne Erde
www.grueneerde.com

There is an almost philosophical basic idea behind the kitchens of Green Earth: to connect modern design with the actual, traditional task of a kitchen—being a room where people like to send time and like to live. All corpuses and fronts of the Jovanella kitchen are therefore designed in high-quality, vivid beech or oak solid wood which has only been treated with oil. And the work tops made of heavy granite from Lower Austria do not only look valuable—they also cope with everything life brings along in a kitchen. A both though and clear as well as reduced design bestow a certain reserve on this kitchen, which is accented and mixed up with strong colored glass elements. Slender stainless steel and wood legs let the massive kitchen sink in twinkle-toed and airy. Energy-saving electrical appliances with cool stainless steel fronts top off Jovanella's understatement appearance and, at the same time, make it a piece of design, which does not only convince visually but also functionally.

Hinter den Küchen von Grüne Erde steht ein beinah philosophischer Grundgedanke: modernes Design zu verbinden mit der eigentlichen, traditionellen Aufgabe einer Küche – ein Raum zu sein, in dem man sich gerne aufhält, in dem man lebt. Korpus und Fronten der Küche Jovanella sind deshalb in hochwertigem, lebendigen Buchen- oder Eichenvollholz gehalten, das nur mit Öl behandelt wurde. Und die Arbeitsplatten aus schwerem niederösterreichischen Granit sehen nicht nur wertvoll aus – sie machen auch alles mit, was das Leben so bringt. Eine ebenso robuste wie klare und reduzierte Formgebung verleiht der Küche eine gewisse Zurückhaltung, die durch kräftige farbige Glaselemente akzentuiert und aufgelockert wird. Schlanke Edelstahl-Holzbeine lassen die massive Holzküche leichtfüßig und luftig wirken. Energiesparende Elektrogeräte mit kühlen Edelstahlfronten runden den Understatement-Auftritt von Jovanella ab. Und machen sie gleichzeitig zu einem Designstück, das nicht nur optisch, sondern auch funktional überzeugt.

Data and Facts	Ecological kitchen series
Energy efficiency | Energieeffizienz	up to A++ in case of refrigerators | bis zu A++ bei den Kühlschränken
Water | Wasser	water-saving dishwashers | wassersparende Geschirrspüler
Technology | Technologie	induction cooker, heat pump technology | Induktionsfelder, Wärmepumpentechnologie
Design | Design	classy in high-quality stainless steel | zurückhaltend in hochwertigem Edelstahl

Ecological kitchen series | AEG / Electrolux

www.aeg-electrolux.de

With the Eco Line, AEG currently offers the largest product range of energy-saving products in the household appliance sector. Hereby, stoves, ovens, steamers, dishwashers and refrigerators of the Eco Line do not only help saving energy but are enriching every kitchen in terms of visual appearance as well. Innovative technologies let appliances do with only little power—and dishwashers with little water as well. Moreover, the handy pre-settings such as the energy-saving hotplate in stoves are an additional way to preserve resources. Induction cookers guarantee that no energy is going to waste. As a supplement, AEG constantly keeps developing economical little auxiliaries such as toasters and kettles, which are preparing snacks or hot water considerably more economical then the large stoves and ovens. And the Eco Line itself does not end at the kitchen door: a correspondingly energy-efficient laundry dryer as well as a economical washing machine top off the collection. It is therefore no wonder that eco pioneer AEG has been honored with the energy Award by the European Union for the reduction of energy consumption in 2007.

Mit der Öko Line hält AEG derzeit das breiteste Sortiment an Energiesparprodukten in der Haushaltsgerätebranche bereit. Dabei helfen die Herde, Backöfen, Dampfgarer, Geschirrspülmaschinen und Kühlschränke der Öko Line nicht nur beim Stromsparen, sondern sind auch optisch eine Bereicherung für jede Küche. Innovative Technologien lassen die Geräte mit wenig Strom – und die Geschirrspüler auch mit wenig Wasser – auskommen. Zudem bieten praktische Voreinstellungen, zum Beispiel die stromsparende Warmhaltestufe bei den Herden, zusätzliche Möglichkeiten, um Ressourcen zu schonen. Und Induktionskochfelder sorgen dafür, dass keine Energie verloren geht. Ergänzend dazu entwickelt AEG auch immer sparsamere kleine Helfer, wie Toaster und Wasserkocher, die kleine Gerichte oder Heißwasser deutlich sparsamer zubereiten als die großen Herde und Öfen. Und die Öko Line selbst endet auch nicht an der Küchentür: Ein entsprechend energieeffizienter Wäschetrockner sowie eine sparsame Waschmaschine runden das Programm ab. Kein Wunder also, dass der Öko-Pionier AEG im Jahr 2007 mit dem Energy Award von der Europäischen Kommission zur Verringerung des Energieverbrauchs ausgezeichnet wurde.

Data and Facts		Erika
Material	Material	beech/oak solid wood, glass, stainless steel | Birkensperrholz laminiert, Glas, Edelstahl
Sustainability	Nachhaltigkeit	durable processing, restrained design | langlebige Verarbeitung, zurückhaltendes Design
Manufacture	Verarbeitung	ecologically oriented workshop | ökologisch ausgerichtete Werkstätte
Fair Trade	Fair Trade	made in Germany | made in Germany

Erika | Nils Holger Moormann

www.moormann.de

Erika stashes everything you need for a coffee- or tea kitchen directly on the wall. Nothing is concealed. On the contrary: Colored panels put all the objects in the right perspective and are subdivided into 23 individual modules, for instance for storing spoons, mugs, for making coffee or tea, supplies racks or utensils for washing up. In addition, another panel serves as a foldaway table. The modules are simply hung up on wall mounted rails—just like in case of a presentation system. The measurements of all panels are designed on an exactly defined system to ensure that every individual number and selection of panels perfectly matches. This innovative and surprising kitchen system is based on the ideas and designs of the Berlin designer team ‚Storno‘, consisting of Henrik Drecker, Katharina Ploog, Sven Ulber and Davide Siciliano. Autodidact Nils Holger Moormann, who is well-known for unconventional interior reduced to the essential in the design scene, realizes the team's ideas in his idyllic, Bavarian production facility with plenty of idealism, lots of respect for nature and under the best possible ecological conditions.

Erika verstaut alles, was in einer Kaffee- bzw. Teeküche gebraucht wird, an der Wand. Hier wird nichts versteckt. Im Gegenteil: Farbige Paneele rücken alle Gegenstände ins rechte Licht und sind in 23 unterschiedliche einzelne Module z.B. für Löffel, Tassen, Kaffee- bzw. Teekochen, Bevorratung oder Spülen aufgeteilt. Ein weiteres Paneel dient als Klapptisch. Die Module werden – ähnlich wie bei einem Präsentationssystem – einfach in Wand-Schienen eingehängt. Die Maße aller Paneele basieren dabei auf einem exakt definierten Raster, so dass jede individuelle Anzahl und Auswahl zusammenpasst. Kreiert wurde dieses neuartige und überraschende Küchensystem von der studentischen Designgruppe Storno aus Berlin – bestehend aus Henrik Drecker, Katharina Ploog, Sven Ulber und Davide Siciliano. Der Autodidakt Nils Holger Moormann, der in der Designszene für eigenwilliges Interieur, reduziert auf das Wesentliche, steht, realisiert die Idee in seiner idyllischen, bayerischen Fertigungsstätte. Mit viel Idealismus, jeder Menge Respekt vor der Natur und unter besten Umweltschutzbedingungen.

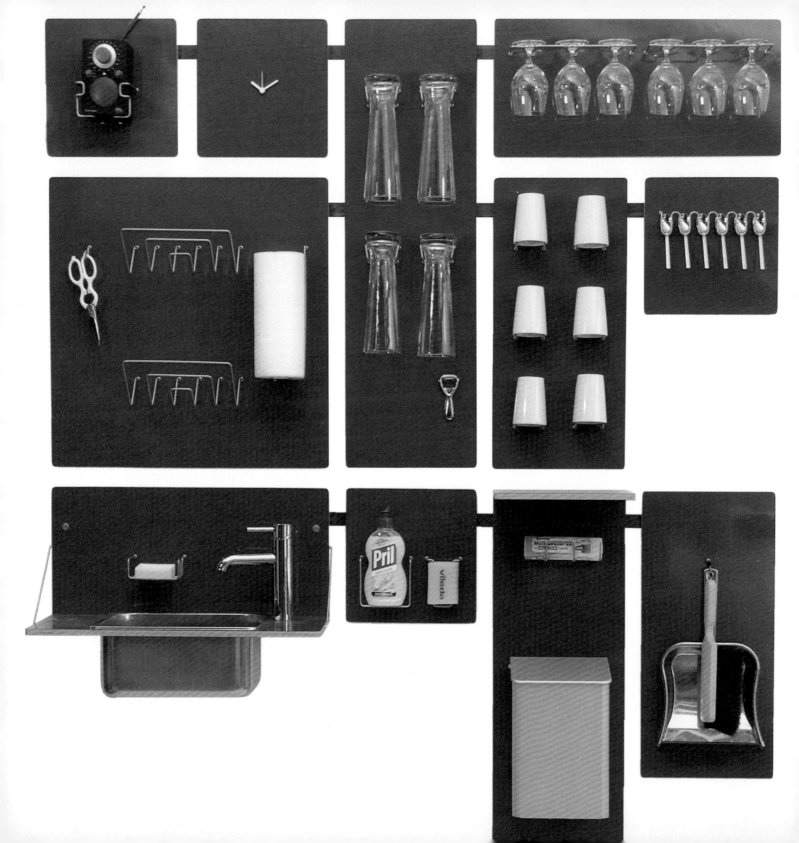

Data and Facts		Presso Coffee Maker
Material | Material		stainless steel | Edelstahl
Sustainability | Nachhaltigkeit		durable processing, timeless Design | langlebige Verarbeitung, zeitloses Design
Technology | Technologie		making coffee without electricity | Kaffeezubereitung ohne Strom

Presso Coffee Maker | Presso

www.presso.co.ok

Coffee currently truly booms. Today's townscapes are almost unimaginable without cafés and coffee shops. And also people at home drink more and more of the black hot beverage. Preparing a pot of coffee consumes a lot of energy every time—so this is also an important aspect to start thinking of some energy efficient, environmentally friendly solutions. The Presso Coffee Maker makes real espresso—and needs no electricity for that. However, one still has to heat up the water, of course but as the Presso Coffee Maker uses hot water from a kettle, this can be effected much more energy-saving than with a traditional coffee machine. The hot water is then conveyed through the machine by manual pressure—with the result being fresh, hot espresso. The simple and functional design in high-quality stainless steel just fits perfectly into every kitchen and coffee bar. It is therefore no wonder that the fancy and eco-correct Presso Coffee Maker with its organically rounded-off shapes has been honored with numerous design awards in the past years.

Kaffee erlebt derzeit einen wahren Boom: Cafés und Coffee Shops sind aus einem Stadtbild heute kaum noch wegzudenken. Und auch zu Hause wird immer mehr von dem schwarzen Heißgetränk getrunken. Jede Zubereitung einer Kanne Kaffee verbraucht eine Menge Energie – ein wichtiger Punkt also, auch hier mit energieeffizienten, umweltfreundlichen Ideen anzusetzen. Der Presso Coffee Maker macht echten Espresso – und das ganz ohne Strom. Natürlich bleibt das Erhitzen des Wassers trotzdem nicht aus, aber mit einem Wasserkocher lässt sich dies deutlich energiesparender erledigen als mit einer klassischen Kaffeemaschine. Per manuellem Druck wird das heiße Wasser dann durch die Maschine befördert – heraus kommt frischer, heißer Espresso. Das schlichte und funktionale Design in hochwertigem Edelstahl macht sich dabei in jeder Küche und Kaffeebar gut. Kein Wunder, dass der schicke und öko-korrekte Presso Coffee Maker mit den organisch abgerundeten Formen in den letzten Jahren mit zahlreichen Designpreisen ausgezeichnet wurde.

Data and Facts		kitchen linee
Material | Material		local hardwoods, glass, stainless steel | heimische Laubhölzer, Glas, Edelstahl
Manufacture | Verarbeitung		natural oils, water-based adhesives | natürliche Öle, wasserbasierte Leime
Sustainability | Nachhaltigkeit		durable processing, classical design | langlebige Verarbeitung, klassisches Design
Technology | Technologie		Servo-Drive | Servo-Drive
Fair Trade | Fair Trade		made in Austria | made in Austria

kitchen linee | TEAM 7
www.team7.at

A linear concept gives kitchen linee of TEAM 7 her name and her very special flair. Therefore, the grain of all massive wood elements used always runs horizontally in order to underline the straight look. Drawers and doors have either no handles at all or flush-fitting handles reaching over the entire width of doors and drawers. And the baseboard detaches the kitchen from the floor in a particularly elegant way. Types of wood such as alder, maple, beech, core beech, cherry or partially walnut are used for the massive wood elements. Elements such as glossy or matt colored glass as well as stainless steel and aluminum guarantee for harmonious contrasts. All materials are selected and processed according to economic and ecologic aspects and do therefore also provide for very natural advantages in use: the natural, oiled wood filters smells and has a bacteria-repressive effect. Foodstuffs remain fresh much longer in the 19 mm strong massive wood corpus—and are particularly tasty in the pure, unobtrusive and highly modern ambience of TEAM 7's line kitchen.

Ein lineares Konzept gibt der Küche linee von TEAM 7 ihren Namen und ihr ganz besonderes Flair. So verläuft die Maserung der Massivholzelemente stets horizontal, um den geradlinigen Look zu unterstreichen. Auf Griffstangen wird entweder vollständig verzichtet oder sie ziehen sich über die komplette Breite der Türen und Schubladen. Und die Sockelblende löst die Küche besonders elegant vom Boden. Bei den Elementen aus Massivholz kommen Erle, Ahorn, Buche, Kernbuche, Kirschbaum oder teilweise Nussbaum zum Einsatz. Harmonische Kontraste entstehen durch Elemente aus glänzendem oder mattem farbigem Glas sowie Edelstahl und Aluminium. Alle Materialien werden nach ökonomischen und ökologischen Gesichtspunkten ausgewählt und weiterverarbeitet. Und bieten so auch im Gebrauch ganz natürliche Vorteile: Das naturbelassene, geölte Holz filtert Gerüche und wirkt bakterienhemmend. Lebensmittel bleiben im 19 mm starken Massivholz-Korpus länger frisch – und schmecken im puren, dezenten und hochmodernen Ambiente der TEAM 7 Küche linee besonders lecker.

Data and Facts		New York, Traffic Recycling Ware
Material	Material	silver 925, recycled traffic signs, copper rivets | Silber 925, Recycelte Verkehrsschilder, Kupfernieten
Design	Design	artistic, individual | künstlerisch, individuell
Sustainability	Nachhaltigkeit	recycled material in durable processing | recyceltes Material in langlebiger Verarbeitung

Bin There!, Flat Truss | Boris Bally

www.borisbally.com

Traffic signs are actually something pretty normal and common. By recycling and well directed appropriation, however, they become exceptional furnishings and household equipment having the character of pieces of art. Boris Bally realizes these ideas in form of chairs, tables, cups, plates and cutlery—all handcrafted, sawn and riveted together of old American traffic signs. In processing, he sticks to the motto of the American Natives "Using all parts of the Bison" and uses the traffic signs—most of them coming from New York—to the tag. In this way it is likely that even the smallest parts, remaining in the production of interior and cutlery, become beautiful jewelry or key rings. With their unique and artful look those ecological and politically correct recycling articles bring some fresh air on a set table. And some international art galleries and design museums have already recognized that—they are presenting Boris Bally's recycling objects as contemporary art of daily use on their exhibition areas.

Verkehrsschilder sind eigentlich etwas ganz normales und alltägliches. Durch Recycling und gezielte Zweckentfremdung werden sie jedoch zu außergewöhnlichen Einrichtungs- und Haushaltsgegenständen mit Objektcharakter. Boris Bally realisiert diese Idee in Form von Stühlen, Tischen, Bechern, Tellern und Besteckgarnituren – alle handmontiert, gesägt und genietet aus alten amerikanischen Verkehrsschildern. Bei der Verarbeitung hält er sich an das Motto der American Natives „Using all parts of the Bison" und verwertet die – größtenteils aus New York stammenden – Verkehrsschilder bis zum letzten Rest. So werden aus Kleinstteilen, die bei der Produktion von Interieur und Geschirr übrig bleiben, auch mal kreative Schmuckstücke oder Schlüsselanhänger. Die ökologisch und politisch korrekten Recyclingartikel bringen mit ihrem einzigartigen, kunstvollen Look frischen Schwung auf den gedeckten Tisch. Und das haben auch internationale Kunstgalerien und Designmuseen bereits erkannt – sie präsentieren Boris Ballys Recycling Objekte als zeitgemäße Gebrauchskunst auf ihren Ausstellungsflächen.

Data and Facts		Hemp Linen
Material	Material		ecologically correct hemp linen | öko-korrektes Hanfgewebe
Manufacture	Verarbeitung		natural, eco-friendly colors | natürliche, umweltfreundliche Farben
Sustainability	Nachhaltigkeit		fast re-growing raw material | schnell nachwachsender Rohstoff
Fair Trade	Fair Trade		made in the United Kingdom | made in United Kingdom

Hemp Linen | Draper's Organic

www.drapersorganic.co.uk

Eco-interests and design requirements do no longer have to clash when it comes to table linen. The table cloths, runners, placemats, napkins and cushions of Draper's Organic are exclusively made of cultivated hemp. No pesticides are used already while the hemp plants are brought up and during the further processing Draper's Organic focuses on natural colors that are not harmful to the environment. For their tablecloth line, the British designers have the rediscovered, traditional hemp thread interwoven to a tough, linen-like structure. This slightly rougher pattern perfectly fits a rather country-house furnishing style and sets interesting contrasts when it meets light glass tables or cool stainless steel. The sustainable textiles are perfectly adapted to individual decoration ideas and furnishing looks by individual embroideries and a wide spectrum of natural colors ranging from light to dark and from soft to strong.

Auch wenn es um Tischtextilien geht, müssen Öko-Interessen und Designansprüche längst nicht mehr kollidieren. Die Tischtücher, Läufer, Platzsets, Servietten und Kissen von Draper's Organic werden ausschließlich aus umweltverträglich angebautem Nutzhanf hergestellt. Bereits in der Aufzucht der Pflanzen kommen hier keinerlei Pestizide zum Einsatz – und in der Weiterverarbeitung setzt Draper's Organic auf natürliche Farben, die die Umwelt nicht belasten. Für ihr Tischwäsche-Programm lassen die britischen Designer das wiederentdeckte, traditionelle Hanfgarn zu einer robusten, Leinen-ähnlichen Struktur verweben. Das etwas gröbere Dessin passt hervorragend zu einem ländlichen Einrichtungsstil. Und setzt interessante Kontraste, wenn es auf leichte Glastische oder kühlen Edelstahl trifft. Perfekt angepasst an persönliche Deko-Ideen und Einrichtungslooks werden die nachhaltigen Textilien durch individuelle Stickereien und ein breitgefächertes Naturfarbspektrum von hell bis dunkel sowie von sanft bis kräftig.

Data and Facts	Serving & More
Manufacture | Produktion	high environmental standards, environmentally friendly waste disposal, recycling | hohe Umweltstandards, umweltverträgliche Müllentsorgung, Recycling
Energy | Energie	from company-own solar cells | aus hauseigenen Solarzellen
Sustainability | Nachhaltigkeit	fast re-growing raw material | schnell nachwachsender Rohstoff
Social commitment | Soziales Engagement	regional projects | regionale Projekte
Fair Trade | Fair Trade	made in Germany | made in Germany

Serving & More | Schott Zwiesel

www.schott-zwiesel.de

When food is served on clear Tritan ® Crystal glass, it is a treat for all senses. The lines Arrondi, Folio, Lagoon and Lavinia from Serving & More of Schott Zwiesel enable for exactly that in a particularly elegant way: clear and simple design do not distract from the tempting food but underlines the high value of the fresh and perfectly prepared food with its sparkling structure. Bowls and plates are just perfect for serving various dips, salads, desserts or starters. And the highlights of every menu all find their places on beautiful etageres. In the production of those precious pieces for the set table, the rich in tradition glassworks in Zwiesel focuses on the most state-of-the-art ecological aspects and it goes therefore without saying that energy production with solar power is more and more integrated in the production plant's energy plan. Moreover, the Bavarian glass artists also set new standards in terms of an environmentally friendly waste disposal.

Wenn Speisen auf klarem Tritan® Kristallglas serviert werden, ist das ein Genuss für alle Sinne. Die Serien Arrondi, Folio, Lagoon und Lavinia aus dem Bereich Serving & More von Schott Zwiesel ermöglichen genau dies auf besonders elegante Weise: Schlichte, klare Formen lenken nicht von der verführerischen Mahlzeit ab, sondern unterstreichen mit ihrer funkelnden Struktur den hohen Wert der herrlich frischen oder ansprechend zubereiteten Nahrung. Schalen und Teller eignen sich perfekt zum Reichen verschiedener Dips, Salate, Desserts oder Vorspeisen. Und die Highlights eines Menüs finden auf auffälligen Etageren ihren Platz. Bei der Herstellung dieser Schmuckstücke für die gedeckte Tafel setzt die traditionsreiche Zwieseler Glashütte auf modernste ökologische Aspekte. So ist es eine Selbstverständlichkeit, die Energiegewinnung mit Solarkraft immer mehr in den bestehenden Energiehaushalt der Produktionsstätten zu integrieren. Und auch bei der umweltverträglichen Müllentsorgung setzen die bayerischen Glaskünstler Maßstäbe.

Data and Facts		EcoWare
Material | Material		bamboo, bio-degradable plastic | Bambus, biologisch abbaubarer Kunstsstoff
Evidence of suitability | Entsorgbarkeit		completely recyclable | komplett recycelbar
Manufacture | Produktion		innovative material composition | innovative Materialkomposition

EcoWare | Tom Dixon

www.tomdixon.net

Bio-degradable plastic combined with solid bamboo—that sounds like a daring mixture for up-market designer tableware. Tom Dixon's Eco Ware proves that such a courageous environmental idea can look refreshingly different and surprisingly elegant at the same time. The black-brown plates, bowls and cups attract attention because of their extraordinary color. Innovative shapes such as the cross-leg at the bottom of the cup and bowl line show that even environmentally-conscious design is able to set trends. The new, sustainable material of Tom Dixon's Eco Ware is produced by mixing natural bamboo fibers with water-based plastic polymers. And this combination does not only look good in practical use but is also extremely tough, robust and heat-resistant. And should the fancy, functional Eco Ware tableware really be disused at some stage it can be disposed off on the compost to be recycled in the natural decomposition cycle.

Biologisch abbaubares Plastik kombiniert mit massivem Bambus – das klingt erst einmal nach einer waghalsigen Mischung für edles Designergeschirr. Die Eco Ware von Tom Dixon zeigt, dass solch eine mutige Umweltidee wunderbar anders und gleichzeitig überraschend elegant aussehen kann. Die schwarz-braun melierten Teller, Schüsseln und Becher ziehen schon allein wegen ihrer außergewöhnlichen Farbgebung alle Blicke auf sich. Und innovative Formen wie der stützende Kreuzfuß am Boden der Becher- und Schüsselserie zeigen, dass auch umweltbewusstes Design Trends setzen kann. Das neuartige, nachhaltige Material der Tom Dixon Eco Ware wird durch eine Vermengung natürlicher Bambusfasern mit wasserbasierten Plastikpolymeren hergestellt. Im Gebrauch sieht es dann nicht nur gut aus, es ist auch extrem robust, widerstandsfähig sowie hitzebeständig. Und hat das schicke, funktionale Eco Geschirr dann doch irgendwann einmal ausgedient, kann es ganz einfach auf dem Kompost dem natürlichen Zersetzungskreislauf zugeführt und damit entsorgt werden.

Data and Facts		Free Spirit
Material	Material	porcelain | Porzellan
Evidence of suitability	Entsorgbarkeit	completely recyclable | komplett recycelbar
Manufacture	Produktion	energy-saving and resource-sound, environmentally conscious | energie- und ressourcenschonend, umweltbewusst
Fair Trade	Fair Trade	made in Germany | made in Germany
Design	Design	inspired by nature | von der Natur inspiriert

Free Spirit | Rosenthal

www.rosenthal.de

Rosenthal has always been working with lots of respect for man, ecology and nature. This is why things like most state-of-the-art filter systems, a gentle to resources and energy-saving way of working as well as social labor conditions go without saying for this highly modern company with a long tradition. With so much ecological and human commitment it does not come as a surprise that nature also has her when it comes to designing dinnerware collections—for instance in case of the multiply awarded design of the porcelain service Free Spirit. This is where organic form language and symmetry dissolve into an innovative form with functional aspiration and expressive design. Free Spirit unlocks creative space for distinctive mixing, matching and experimenting. The basis of this boundlessly variable porcelain and glass collection are the square and rectangular plates and platters of different sizes and depths whose organic form language is emphasized by a particularly thin porcelain body. Robin Platt, an international renowned designer and one of the outstanding representatives of the new British design, has created a perfect collection for Rosenthal which continues in the formally matching drinking-glass collection.

Die Marke Rosenthal arbeitet seit jeher mit viel Respekt vor Mensch, Umwelt und Natur. Deshalb sind modernste Filteranlagen, ressourcenschonendes und energiesparendes Arbeiten sowie soziale Arbeitsbedingungen eine Selbstverständlichkeit für das hochmoderne Traditionsunternehmen. Bei so viel ökologischem und menschlichem Engagement verwundert es dann nicht, dass auch bei der Formgebung von Geschirrkollektionen die Natur ihren Beitrag leistet – wie bei dem mehrfach ausgezeichneten Design des Porzellanservices Free Spirit. Hier verschmelzen organische Formensprache und Symmetrie zu einer innovativen Form mit funktionalem Anspruch und ausdrucksstarkem Design. Free Spirit eröffnet damit kreative Freiräume zum individuellen Kombinieren und Experimentieren. Die Grundlage der vielfältig zu kombinierenden Porzellan- und Glaskollektion bilden dabei quadratische und rechteckige Teller und Platten unterschiedlicher Größe und Tiefe, deren organische Formsprache durch einen besonders dünnen Porzellanscherben betont wird. Der international bekannte Designer Robin Platt – er zählt zu den herausragenden Vertretern des neuen britischen Designs – hat damit für Rosenthal eine Kollektion erschaffen, die sich bis in die formal passende Trinkglas-Kollektion fortsetzt.

Data and Facts		Tray Up, Dishtowel Loop
Material	Material	Wood/Linoleum, half-linen | Holz/Linoleum, Halbleinen
Design	Design	simple, functional | schlicht, funktional
Fair Trade	Fair Trade	produced in German workshops for handicapped people | produziert in deutschen Behindertenwerkstätten
Designawards	Designpreise	#FORM 2002/2008, DesignPlus 2003/2007 | #FORM 2002/2008, DesignPlus 2003/2007

Tray Up, Dishtowel Loop | side by side

www.sidebyside-design.de

Demanding design products produced by physically or mentally handicapped persons—is that possible? It is! And uncountable design awards already in the first years after the brand has been founded prove it. Quality and design must be convincing—with this goal in mind, the first side by side collection has been presented in 2002. Created by 20 dedicated designers and realized in 9 different workshops for handicapped people, the side by side design articles are today making their way all over the world. For instance, the tray UP by Konrad Weinhuber: the tray's flexible edge can be folded up to carry it and folded down to place it on the table. Made of local maple and heat-resistant laminate, it does not only look quite fancy but is also particularly versatility usable. Another example is dish towel Loop by the designer team Olze & Wilkens. The towels' fancy half-linen is tough, haptically comfortable and extremely absorbent. And the lines and flowers printed on it lead the way to the hanger made of red cord—unique design which makes life a bit easier after all.

Anspruchsvolle Designprodukte, hergestellt von Menschen mit körperlicher und geistiger Behinderung, geht das überhaupt? Es geht, was unzählige Designpreise allein in den ersten Jahren seit Markengründung beweisen. Qualität und Design müssen überzeugen – mit diesem Anspruch wurde 2002 die erste side by side Kollektion präsentiert. Entworfen von 20 engagierten Designern und realisiert in neun verschiedenen Werkstätten für behinderte Menschen gehen die side by side Designartikel heute ihren Weg in die ganze Welt. Wie das Tablett UP von Designer Konrad Weinhuber: Dessen flexibler Tablettrand ist zum Tragen nach oben und am Tisch nach unten geklappt. Gefertigt aus heimischem Ahorn und hitzebeständigem Laminat sieht es nicht nur schick aus – es ist auch besonders vielseitig einsetzbar. Oder die Geschirrtücher Loop vom Designerteam Olze & Wilkens. Ihr edles Halbleinen ist strapazierfähig, haptisch angenehm und extrem saugfähig. Und die im Siebdruck aufgebrachten Linien und Blumen weisen den Weg zum Aufhänger aus roter Tuchschnur – einzigartiges Design, das ganz nebenbei auch noch das Leben ein bisschen einfacher macht.

Data and Facts		Wine & Bar
Manufacture	Produktion	high environmental standards, eco-friendly waste disposal, recycling | hohe Umweltstandards, umweltverträgliche Müllentsorgung, Recycling
Energy	Energie	from company-own solar cells | aus hauseigenen Solarzellen
Sustainability	Nachhaltigkeit	fast re-growing raw material | schnell nachwachsender Rohstoff
Social commitment	Soziales Engagement	regional projects | regionale Projekte
Fair Trade	Fair Trade	made in Germany | made in Germany

Wine & Bar | Schott Zwiesel
www.schott-zwiesel.de

The quality of a refreshing, tasty drink is significantly living from the glass. The glasses for Wine and Bar of Schott Zwiesel let real gourmet pleasures evolve. Lines such as Fine, Gentle Glow, Pure Loop or Wine Basic emphasize the transparency of liquids especially well. Perfect designs give wines room to open up their rich aromas and flavors. The modern, elegant designs provide for a cool look at the table at one time, and a rather classic look at the other time. The innovative and international patented Tritan® Crystal glass gives our gentle glasses a high level of brilliance and makes them break, scratch and dishwasher resistant. The result is a high longevity which exactly corresponds to the company's philosophy regarding ecology and sustainability. After all, Schott Zwiesel focuses on renewable energy from solar cells already in production. The solar cells are produced by the company itself. Another important aspect of Schott Zwiesel is social justice which is lived towards employees and families, health, environment, science and society.

Die Qualität eines erfrischenden, leckeren Getränks lebt maßgeblich vom Glas. Die Trinkgläser für Wein und Bar von Schott Zwiesel bringen echten Gourmetgenuss zur Entfaltung. Serien wie Fine, Gentle Glow, Pure Loop oder Wine Basic bringen die Transparenz von Flüssigkeiten besonders gut zur Geltung. Perfekte Formen geben zarten Aromen Raum zur Entfaltung. Und modern-elegante Designs sorgen bei Tisch für einen mal coolen, mal eher klassischen Look. Das innovative und international patentierte Tritan® Kristallglas macht die zarten Gläser dabei in hohem Maße brillant, bruch- und kratzfest sowie spülmaschinenfest. Daraus resultiert eine hohe Langlebigkeit, die der Firmenphilosophie von Umweltschutz und Nachhaltigkeit genau entspricht. Schließlich setzt Schott Zwiesel bereits in der Produktion auf erneuerbare Energien aus Solarzellen, die sie selbst produzieren. Ein weiterer wichtiger Unternehmensaspekt von Schott Zwiesel ist soziale Gerechtigkeit, die gegenüber Mitarbeitern und Familien, Gesundheit, Umwelt, Wissenschaft und Gesellschaft gelebt wird.

Data and Facts		Recycling Teasets
Material	Material	recycled, old tea sets	recycelte, alte Teeservice
Manufacture	Verarbeitung	environmentally compatible, food safe colors	umweltverträgliche, lebensmittelechte Farben
Fair Trade	Fair Trade	made in United Kingdom	made in United Kingdom
Designawards	Designpreise	Peter Walker Award, 2007	Peter Walker Award, 2007

Recycling Teasets | Christine Misiak

www.christinemisiak.co.uk

Lots of old things are just tossed although they could be well used. Just like old tea sets whose look is not exactly modern indeed, but that are not broken yet. And this is exactly what Christine Misiak made her mission under consideration of recycling and sustainability aspects and transforms them into funny up-to-date designer pieces with lots of love for details and flashy pop-colors. This is why there are now porcelain services with designs of the past in colors of the present—finished with eco-friendly and food safe colors, of course. Other old tea sets used to be made of porcelain with silver handles and spouts. If that porcelain is broken, Christine Misiak just replaces it by newly fired, clear forms which she dips into striking loud colors as well. She then refits the silver elements—and ready are the sets called Old/ New or New/ Old Tea Sets. She also finishes old metal tea sets with refreshing colors and new elements such as straight solid wood handles.

Viele alte Dinge werden einfach weggeworfen, obwohl sie noch gut zu gebrauchen wären. Wie alte Teeservice, deren Look zwar nicht mehr ganz zeitgemäß ist, die aber noch nicht kaputt sind. Genau die hat sich Christine Misiak unter dem Aspekt von Recycling und Nachhaltigkeit vorgenommen und sie mit viel Liebe zum Detail sowie jeder Menge Mut zu knalligen Pop-Farben in witzige Up-to-date-Designerstücke verwandelt. So gibt es nun Porzellanservice mit der Form von anno dazumal in den Farben von heute – lackiert natürlich mit umweltverträglichen und lebensmittelechten Farben. Weitere alte Teeservice bestanden einmal aus Porzellan mit silbernen Griffen und Ausgießern. Ist das Porzellan davon kaputt, ersetzt Christine Misiak dies durch neu gebrannte, klare Formen, die sie ebenfalls in auffällig knallige Farben taucht. Die silbernen Elemente bringt sie dann wieder an – und fertig sind die Service, die Old-New-beziehungsweise New-Old-Sets heißen. Auch alte Tea Sets aus Metall bearbeitet sie mit erfrischenden Farben und neuen Elementen wie geradlinigen Massivholzgriffen.

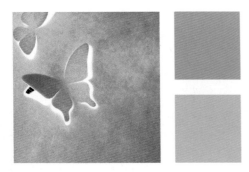

Data and Facts		Coron, Delight, Kimono	
Material | Material		natural, bio-degradable woolen felt | natürlicher, biologisch abbaubarer Wollfilz	
Manufacture | Verarbeitung		environmentally compatible colors | umweltverträgliche Farben	
Fair Trade | Fair Trade		made in the United Kingdom | made in United Kingdom	
Designers | Designers		co-operations with MoMA-Shop, Louvre-Shop, Paul Smith | Kooperationen u.a. mit MoMA-Shop, Louvre-Shop, Paul Smith	

Coron, Delight, Kimono | Mixko

www.mixko.co.uk

Wool felt is a natural material with a century old tradition. The material has an insulating effect and improves room climate—it is therefore perfect to design high-quality accessories with it. The British-Japanese designer duo Mixko uses felt in case of Kimono to keep wine bottles perfectly tempered. The bio-degradable and with natural colors dyed felt insulates the bottle temperature and also catches some droplets of wine thanks to its high absorbent power. Another outstanding characteristic of this flex-leveled fabric is that it is flameproof which makes it just the perfect material for a lamp shade. In case of the unobtrusive model Coron, a piece of felt is simply held together by a wooden button—a simple idea that surprises and inspires with its simplicity. Delight, however, comes along a bit friskier. The tender, punched out butterflies adds the heavy felt an airy sleaziness. And last but not least, the strong colors give the traditional winter material felt a rather summerly, fresh touch.

Wollfilz ist ein natürliches Material mit jahrhundertealter Tradition. Das Material wirkt isolierend und es verbessert das Raumklima – ideal also, um damit hochwertige Wohnaccessoires zu designen. Das britisch-japanische Designerduo Mixko nutzt bei Kimono den Filz, um Weinflaschen ideal temperiert zu halten. Der biologisch abbaubare und mit natürlichen Farben gefärbte Filz isoliert die Flaschentemperatur und schluckt dank seiner hohen Saugkraft auch noch ein Tröpfchen Wein, das vielleicht einmal daneben geht. Eine weitere herausragende Eigenschaft des gewalkten Stoffes ist es, nicht entflammbar zu sein. Deshalb eignet er sich hervorragend als Lampenschirm. Bei dem dezent-zurückhaltenden Modell Coron wird dafür ein Filztuch von einem Holzknopf zusammengehalten – eine simple Idee, die mit ihrer Einfachheit überrascht und begeistert. Delight hingegen kommt etwas verspielter daher. Die zarten, ausgestanzten Schmetterlinge geben dem schweren Filz eine luftige Leichtigkeit. Und kräftige Farben lassen das klassische Wintermaterial Filz sommerlich frisch wirken.

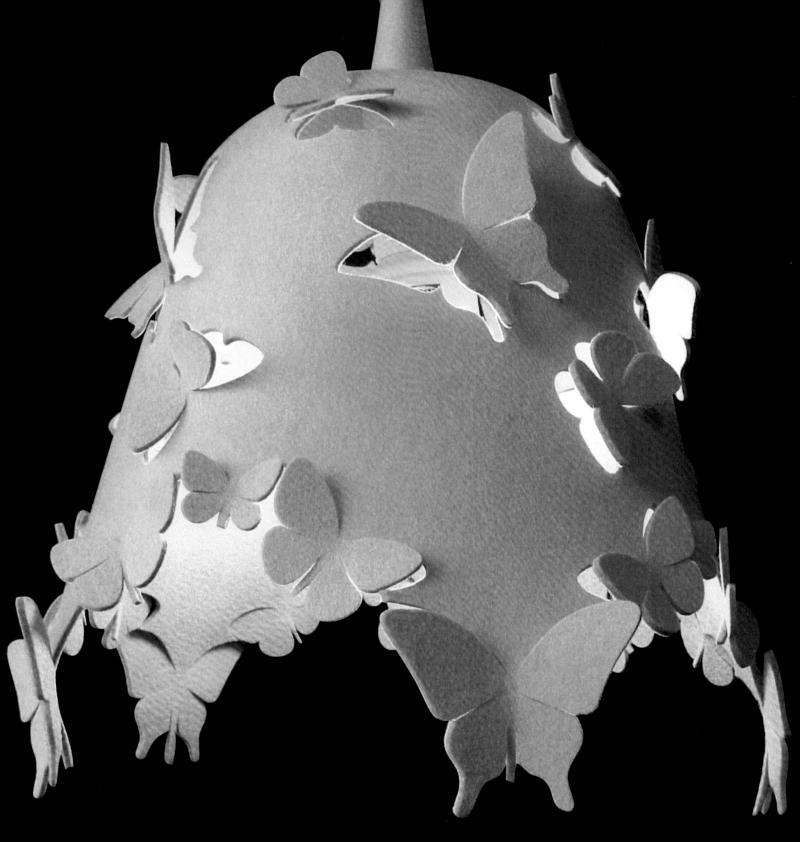

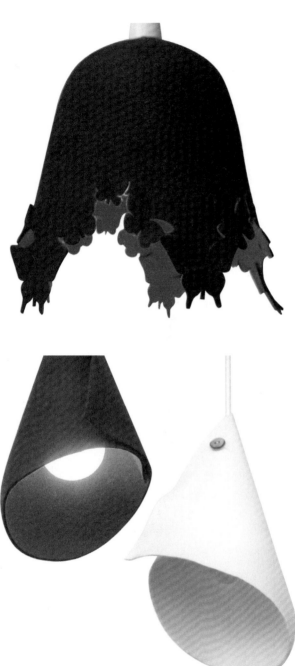

Data and Facts		Bowls
Material	Material		Macadamia nut shells, plastic | Macadamia-Nussschalen, Kunststoff
Manufacture	Verarbeitung		natural Macadamia oil as finish | natürliches Macadamia-Öl als Finish
Fair Trade	Fair Trade		made in Australia | made in Australia

Bowls | husque
www.husque.com

When buying peeled or salted, tasty macadamia nuts, one is not exactly wondering what happens to the shells. The Australian designer Marc Harrison posed himself exactly this question—and thus discovered a valuable raw material: in Australia, the home of the macadamia nut, 43,000 tons of macadamia are harvested and processed including its shell every year. While the kernels are popular all over the world, their shells are mostly disposed off. Marc Harrison now assigned a specific use to the shells and produces wonderful, simple and, at the same time, peculiar fruit and deco bowls. Therefore, the shells of the macadamia nut are finely milled in the first place and then processed with a special plastic polymer producing a material from which new, large bowls are being made. These partially remain natural and untreated and are partially finished—and finally polished with natural macadamia oil until they shine like precious satin.

Beim Kauf von geschälten und gesalzenen, leckeren Macadamia-Nüssen fragt man sich nicht unbedingt, was nun mit all den Schalen passiert. Der australische Designer Marc Harrison hat sich genau diese Frage gestellt – und so einen wertvollen Rohstoff entdeckt: In Australien, der Heimat der Macadamia-Nuss, werden jährlich etwa 43.000 Tonnen Macadamia inklusive Schalen geerntet und verarbeitet. Während die Kerne auf der ganzen Welt geliebt werden, werden die Schalen meist entsorgt. Marc Harrison hat dafür nun eine Verwendung gefunden und produziert wunderbar schlichte und zugleich auffällige Obstschüsseln und Dekoschälchen daraus. Dazu werden die Schalen der Macadamia-Nuss erst einmal fein zermahlen. Im Anschluss wird das entstandene Mehl mit einem speziellen Kunststoff-Polymer vermengt, so dass ein Material entsteht, aus dem neue, große Schalen geformt werden können. Diese werden teilweise natürlich belassen und teilweise lackiert – und zu guter Letzt mit natürlichem Macadamia-Öl so lange poliert, bis sie wie edler Satin schimmern.

Data and Facts		tranSglass
Material	Material		recycling glass | Recycling Glas
Disposability	Entsorgbarkeit		completely recyclable | komplett recycelbar
Design	Design		each piece is unique | jedes Stück ein Unikat
Fair Trade	Fair Trade		co-operation with Aid to Artisans in Guatemala | Kooperation mit Aid to Artisans in Guatemala

tranSglass | Artecnica Inc

www.artecnicainc.com

Old, disused bottles either ending up at drink retailers against pledge, at the bottle bank—or at Artecnica Inc. Designers Emma Woffenden & Tord Boontje had the idea to not just throw old wine, water or other bottles away but to produce new items by processing them with special polishing techniques, targeted cutting and creative joining. The products of the TranSglass collection range from funny vases over individual candle holders, culminating in noble carafes and matching tumblers. Those extraordinary pieces are produced in co-operation with the organization Aid to Artisans by Guatemalan artisans and craftsmen. These are able to bring in their traditional technical skills of glass within this project—and work under socially correct labor conditions, in human conditions and for an appropriate, fair salary.

Alte Flaschen, die ausgedient haben, landen entweder gegen Pfand beim Getränkehändler, im Altglascontainer – oder bei Artecnica Inc. Die Designer Emma Woffenden & Tord Boontje kamen hier auf die Idee, alte Wein-, Wasser- oder sonstige Getränkeflaschen aus Glas nicht einfach wegzuwerfen. Sondern durch spezielle Poliertechniken, durch gezieltes Zerschneiden und durch kreatives Aneinanderfügen neue Gegenstände entstehen zu lassen. Die Produkte, die bei der Serie TranSglass aus alten Flaschen entstehen, reichen von witzigen Vasen über individuelle Kerzenständer bis hin zur edlen Karaffe und den dazugehörigen Trinkbechern. Produziert werden die außergewöhnlichen Stücke in Kooperation mit der Organisation Aid to Artisans von guatemaltekischen Künstlern und Handwerkern. Diese können im Rahmen des Projekts ihr traditionelles, handwerkliches Geschick im Umgang mit Glas einbringen – und arbeiten dafür unter sozialen Arbeitsbedingungen, in menschlichen Verhältnissen und für eine angemessene, faire Vergütung.

Data and Facts	Mixed Tableware
Design | Design	innovative mixture of tradition and modern design | Innovativer Mix aus Tradition und Moderne
Fair Trade | Fair Trade	co-operation with SAI (Social Accountability International), no child labor guaranteed, Fair Trade Project in Madagascar | Kooperation mit SAI (Social Accountability International), garantiert keine Kinderarbeit, Fair Trade Projekt in Madagaskar

Mixed Tableware | rice
www.rice.dk

Design for big and small with a clear mission: people care, we care. This is why rice products are designed and developed in Denmark, and are produced by people in the Third World within a Fair Trade Project. All production sites provide for human labor conditions and child labor is not tolerated by rice. It goes without saying that any directives regarding environmental protection are complied with. Moreover, employee's salaries in the workshops are above average. The colored Melamine tableware produced here spreads happiness among the entire family in everyday life: it is unbreakable, hygienic and stylish, looks fantastic and goes through anything. The design which are mainly inspired by traditional tableware, seem innovative due to their fruity candy colors. Good examples for this are the bowls reminding people in grandma's old stirring bowls. The product range also includes cups which are geared to traditional paper cups or soup bowls which already disclose their reminiscence in their names: the Granny Style Melamine Soup Bowls.

Design für Groß und Klein mit einer klaren Mission: Den Menschen soll es gut gehen. Deshalb werden rice Produkte in Dänemark designt und dann von Menschen in der Dritten Welt im Rahmen eines Fair Trade Projekts produziert. In den Produktionsstätten herrschen menschenfreundliche Arbeitsbedingungen, Kinderarbeit wird bei rice nicht geduldet. Die Einhaltung von Umweltschutzrichtlinien ist eine Selbstverständlichkeit. Und die Arbeiter in den Werkstätten werden überdurchschnittlich gut bezahlt. Das knallig bunte Melamin Geschirr, das dabei entsteht, bereitet im Alltag dann der ganzen Familie Freude: es ist robust, hygienisch und stylish, sieht hervorragend aus und macht alles mit. Die Formen, die sich größtenteils an traditionellem Geschirr anlehnen, wirken in den fruchtigen Bonbonfarben innovativ, wie die Schüsseln, die an Omas alte Rührschüsseln erinnern. Becher, die sich an klassischen Pappbechern orientieren. Oder Suppenteller, die ihre Reminiszenz bereits in ihrem Namen preisgeben: die Granny Style Melamine Soup Bowls.

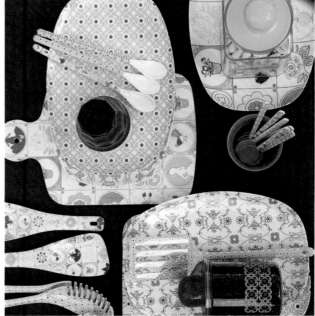

3

4

5

Data and Facts		Bel Air
Material | Material		glass, aluminum, plastics | Glas, Aluminium, Kunststoff
Filter | Filter		natural filter (plant) | Natürlicher Filter (Pflanze)
Sustainability | Nachhaltigkeit		resource-friendly cleaning of air | Ressourcenschonende Reinigung der Luft

O, Local River, Bel Air | Mathieu Lehanneur

www.mathieulehanneur.com

Clean air is especially important in places where food is prepared and eaten. It is a matter of fact, however, that the air inside the house is never as clean as outside. And this is exactly where Mathieu Lehanneur's air filter system Bel Air comes into play: the filter brings a piece of nature from the outside to the inside—and thus improves the room climate very well directed. Included in a futuristic object made of glass, aluminum and plastic, a plant acts as a living filter for air pollution and bad smells. Thanks to an intelligent and well thought through system, the bad air is conducted to the plant, cleaned and led back to the room. Prototype Local River which has been designed by Mathieu Lehanneur in cooperation with Antony van den Bossche is an advanced development stage that generates its very own cycle according to this principle. Hereby, a filter system connects the plant with a tank containing water and living creatures. Due to the special separation and the dependency from each other at the same time, a fascinating, alienating appearance with the unique character of a piece of art is being created.

Gerade dort, wo gekocht und gegessen wird, ist frische, saubere Luft besonders wichtig. Fakt ist jedoch, dass die Luft im Haus nie so rein ist wie die Luft draußen. Das Luftfiltersystem „O" setzt dabei auf Sauerstoffzufuhr während Mathieu Lehanneur bei Bel Air gleich ein Stück Natur von draußen nach drinnen holt – und so gezielt das Raumklima verbessert. Eingeschlossen in ein futuristisches Objekt aus Glas, Aluminium und Plastik, fungiert eine Pflanze als lebender Filter für Luftverschmutzung und schlechte Gerüche. Durch ein ausgeklügeltes System wird die schlechte Luft der Pflanze zugeführt und gereinigt wieder an den Raum abgegeben. Eine Weiterentwicklung, die einen ganz eigenen Kreislauf erzeugt, ist der Prototyp Local River, den Mathieu Lehanneur zusammen mit Anthony van den Bossche designt hat. Dabei verbindet ein Filtersystem die pflanzliche Komponente mit einem Aquarium, das Wasser und Lebewesen beheimatet. Durch die räumliche Trennung und gleichzeitige Abhängigkeit voneinander entsteht eine faszinierende, fremd anmutende Erscheinung mit einzigartigem Objektcharakter.

Data and Facts		sit down, sit & eat
Material | Material		local woods | heimische Hölzer
Manufacture | Verarbeitung		natural oils, waxes | natürliche Öle, Wachse
Production | Produktion		resource-friendly and energy-saving production | ressourcen- und energiesparende Fertigung
Social commitment | Soziales Engagement		well-directed integration of long-time and problematic unemployed | gezielte Integration von Langzeit- und Problemarbeitslosen

sit down, sit & eat | Loft & Lounge

www.loftandlounge.de

One feels home where one sits, eats, laughs and drinks. The seating furniture collection sit&eat by loft&lounge is therefore more than just a piece of furniture—it is a place of hospitality, communication and enjoyment. It combines puristic, innovative design with solidness, impressive unsophistication and lots of space to be comfortable, of course. According to the motto „traditional woods rediscovered", oak, nut and cherry form the natural and untreated basis of modern, individual tables, stools, benches and chairs. loft&lounge always keeps an eye on respect towards nature during the entire development process of these exceptional solid wood furniture: therefore, loft&lounge exclusively buys regional woods with short ways of transport and exactly documented origin. In this way, every customer gets to know exactly where the wood, his table or bench is made of, comes from. In further processing, an energy-saving production and natural treatment go without saying. Moreover, social responsibility is capitalized in the Bavarian production site by owner Johannes Köberl and designer Michael Beck by consequently integrating long-time and problematic unemployed.

Wo man sitzt, isst, lacht und trinkt, dort fühlt man sich zu Hause. Die Sitzmöbelcollection sit&eat von loft&lounge ist deshalb mehr als nur Mobiliar: ein Ort der Gastfreundschaft, der Kommunikation und des Genusses. Sie vereint puristisches, innovatives Design mit robuster Massivität, beeindruckender Natürlichkeit und natürlich mit jeder Menge Platz zum Wohlfühlen. Nach dem Motto „traditionelle Hölzer neu entdeckt" bilden Eiche, Nussbaum und Kirschbaum die naturbelassene Basis von modernen, individuellen Tischen, Hockern, Bänken und Stühlen. Dabei hat loft&lounge während des kompletten Entwicklungsprozesses der außergewöhnlichen Massivholzmöbel den Respekt gegenüber der Natur stets im Blick: so werden Hölzer nur regional eingekauft, mit kurzen Transportwegen und exakt dokumentierter Herkunft. Auf diese Weise erfährt jeder Kunde ganz genau, woher das Holz kommt, aus dem sein Tisch oder seine Bank geschnitzt ist. In der Weiterverarbeitung ist eine energiesparende Produktion und natürliche Behandlung eine Selbstverständlichkeit. Und zudem wird in der bayerischen Fertigungsstätte von Inhaber Johannes Köberl und Designer Michael Beck soziale Verantwortung groß geschrieben: mit der konsequenten Integration von Langzeit- und Problemarbeitslosen.

Data and Facts	Glass deco fabrics
Material	Material	glass made of natural quartz sand	Glas aus natürlichem Quarzsand
Certification	Zertifizierung	Eco-Tex Standard 100	Öko-Tex Standard 100
Design	Design	flexible, individual designs	flexible, individuelle Gestaltungsmöglichkeiten

Glass deco fabrics | Bündnis für Glasdekogewebe

www.glasdekogewebe.de

Glass deco fabric is an innovative material to design walls—and it is just perfectly suitable for kitchens or dining areas as it prevents cracks from reaching the wall surfaces and is resistant to scratches and fire. Moreover, it can be wiped clean and be disinfected easily. The material is mainly manufactured from natural quartz sand. It is absolutely harmless for health and just perfect for a pleasant, cozy and hygienic room climate. Glass deco fabric is ecologically exemplary and certified according to Eco-Tex Standard 100 and moreover carries the signet „Textile Trust". Due to various ways of designing, glass deco fabric enables bringing textile structures, surprising motives or individual patterns to the walls. As glass deco fabric is magnetic, entire walls can also be used as presentation area—without any rails, pin boards or nails. Eventually, every wall coloration which matches the interior concept best is possible as walls can be painted over in any color.

Glasdekogewebe ist ein innovatives Material um Wände zu gestalten – und gerade für Küche und Essbereich eignet es sich besonders gut. Denn es wirkt armierend gegen Risse in der Wand, ist widerstandsfähig gegen Kratzer und feuerfest. Glasdekogewebe lässt sich gründlich reinigen und desinfizieren. Das Material besteht zum größten Teil aus natürlichem Quarzsand. Es ist absolut unschädlich für die Gesundheit und ideal für ein angenehmes, gemütliches und hygienisches Raumklima. Glasdekogewebe ist ökologisch vorbildlich und nach Öko-Tex Standard 100 zertifiziert. Es führt zudem das Signet „Textiles Vertrauen". Durch unterschiedliche Gestaltungen können mit Glasdekogewebe textile Strukturen auf die Wände gebracht werden, überraschende Motive oder individuelle Muster. Das magnetische Glasdekogewebe macht es möglich, ganze Wände als Präsentationsflächen zu nutzen – ohne Schienen, Pinnwände oder Nägel. Und durch farbiges Überstreichen ist jede Wandcoloration möglich, die am Besten zum jeweiligen Interieurkonzept passt.

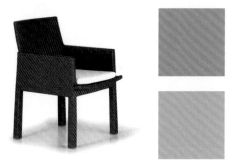

Data and Facts	Spa, Soho
Material | Material	eco-friendly Dedon fiber | umweltfreundliche Dedon-Faser
Sustainability | Nachhaltigkeit	longevity, weather-resistant, timeless design | Langlebigkeit, Witterungsbeständigkeit, zeitloses Design
Fair Trade | Fair Trade	production within a Fair Trade Project on the island of Cebu | Produktion im Rahmen eines Fair Trade Projekts auf Cebu
Design | Design	innovative, multiply awarded | innovativ, mehrfach ausgezeichnet

Spa, Soho | Dedon

www.dedon.de

All Dedon out- and indoor furniture is made of the Dedon fiber—a highly durable synthetic fiber, which is produced in Germany. The sustainable fiber is eco-friendly, washable, extremely easy to maintain and inured to salt-water, sunlight and high or low temperatures. The furniture itself is manufactured on the Philippine island of Cebu—the mecca for the traditional art of handwaeving. Each and every single piece of furniture is therefore hand-crafted. The result: a work of art that combines highly modern technology from Germany with the traditional experience of the handcrafters on Cebu. According to the philosophy "Only a satisfied employee can invent a comfortable chair", Dedon provides best social standards for handcrafters on the Philippine island of Cebu. Moreover, Dedon supports charity projects on site. Once more, the results can be seen in the outstanding Soho collection: clear lines and clean design make this collection a notedly modern and urban innovation for outdoors and indoors.

Die Dedon Out- und Indoor Möbel werden alle aus der Dedon-Faser gefertigt – einer höchst widerstandsfähigen Kunststofffaser, die in Deutschland hergestellt wird. Die nachhaltige Faser ist umweltfreundlich, abwaschbar, extrem pflegeleicht und unempfindlich gegen Salzwasser, Sonnenlicht, hohe oder niedrige Temperaturen. Die Möbel selbst werden auf der philippinischen Insel Cebu gefertigt, dem Mekka der traditionellen Flechtkunst. Jedes Möbel ist somit ein handgefertigtes Stück. Das Ergebnis: Ein Kunstwerk, das hochmoderne Technologie aus Deutschland mit der traditionellen Erfahrung der Handwerker auf Cebu verknüpft. Nach dem Motto „Nur ein zufriedener Mitarbeiter kann auch einen bequemen Stuhl erfinden" werden auf der philippinischen Insel den Dedon Handwerkern beste soziale Standards geboten. Zudem investiert Dedon vor Ort in karitative Projekte. Die Kollektion Soho zeigt einmal mehr, welch herausragend designte Möbel dabei herauskommen: Klare Linien und schnörkelloses Design machen diese Sitzmöbelserie zu einer ausgesprochen modernen und urbanen Innovation für Drinnen und Draußen.

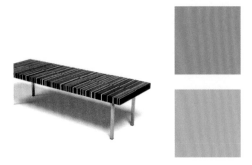

Data and Facts	table 433, chair 777, shelf 114
Material	Material	cardboard | Karton
Sustainability	Nachhaltigkeit	recycling material, which can be recycled itself | Recycling-Material, das selbst wieder recycelt werden kann
Fair Trade	Fair Trade	made in Germany | made in Germany
Design	Design	innovative, partially unique pieces (table 433) | innovativ, teilweise Unikate (table 433)

table 433, chair 777, shelf 114 | diefabrik

www.diefabrik.org

The design office "diefabrik" creates new, unseen pieces of furniture out of old, recycled materials. There are, for instance, pieces like chair 777 and shelf 114 made of cardboard produced of used paper and can be recycled itself. Both pieces of furniture are versatilely useable: The organic design of chair 777 can be turned into the most different positions—and offers a new, different seating everytime. The shelf system shelf 114 consists of individual elements of which everyone can be used as a storage unit itself. The individual parts can also be nested together at their corrugated long sides—and thus make a safe and unusual shelf that can be optionally extended. Table 433 reuses 433 offcuts produced by the wood working industry. At "diefabrik", the individual slats are laminated, shaped and equipped with elegant stainless steel legs. The results are handmade individual items where no table looks like the other.

Das Designbüro diefabrik kreiert neue, ungesehene Möbelstücke aus alten, recycelten Materialien. So bestehen das Sitzmöbel chair 777 und das Regal shelf 114 aus Karton, der aus Altpapier produziert wird und selbst ebenfalls wieder recycelt werden kann. Beide Möbelstücke sind sehr vielseitig einsetzbar: Die organische Form von chair 777 kann in die unterschiedlichsten Positionen gedreht werden – und bietet jedes mal eine neue, andere Sitzgelegenheit. Das Regalsystem shelf 114 besteht aus Einzelelementen, von denen jedes für sich als objektartige Aufbewahrungsgelegenheit genutzt werden kann. Oder die Einzelteile werden an ihren gerippten Längsseiten ineinander gesteckt – und bilden so ein sicheres und ausgefallenes Regal, das beliebig erweitert werden kann. Der Tisch table 433 besteht aus 433 einzelnen Holzstückchen, die als Abfall in der holzverarbeitenden Industrie angefallen sind. Diese Abfallstücke werden bei diefabrik fest miteinander verleimt, in Form gebracht und mit eleganten Edelstahlbeinen verschraubt. So entstehen handgefertigte Einzelstücke, bei denen kein Tisch aussieht wie der andere.

Data and Facts		purelaine airtec picture
Material | Material		keratin canvas | Keratinleinwand
Sustainability | Nachhaltigkeit		cleaning of ambient air from noxious substances | Reinigung der Raumluft von Schadstoffen
Technology | Technologie		unique biological catalyst | einzigartiger biologischer Katalysator

purelaine airtec picture | eco art studio

www.eco-art-studio.de

What sounds unbelievable in the first place is actually possible: a picture on the wall can actively relieve the ambient air from noxious substances. While other standard air cleaners find their places in rooms as ugly gray boxes and only take valuable space, eco art studio breaks new ground here. With the development of the Purelaine Airtec Picture it is actually possible for the first time to hang up an ambient air cleaner just like a picture on the wall. Purelaine Airtec Picture herewith eventually combines healthy living with an appealing ambience. No matter if in the kitchen, the dining room or in other areas of living or life: the Airtec Picture sets noble accents and leaves room for new ideas. Thereby, it's not only the design that impresses but also its unique mode of operation: the picture absorbs noxious substances from the ambient air by means of a special keratin canvas and transforms these into chemically absolutely nontoxic substances. The Purelaine Airtec Picture does hereby not work like a filter but like a biologic catalyst which absorbs noxious and odorous substances such as formaldehyde, ozone, sulfur oxide and nitrogen oxide exclusively by the circulation of ambient air.

Was sich erst einmal unglaublich anhört, ist möglich: Ein Bild an der Wand kann die Raumluft aktiv von Schadstoffen befreien. Während andere handelsübliche Luftreiniger als hässliche graue Kasten in Wohnräumen stehen und nur wertvollen Platz wegnehmen, geht eco art studio hier neue Wege. Mit der Entwicklung des Purelaine Airtec Picture ist es erstmals möglich, einen Raumluftreiniger einfach wie ein Bild an die Wand zu hängen. Purelaine Airtec Picture verbindet damit endlich gesundes Leben mit einem ansprechenden Ambiente. Ob in der Küche, im Esszimmer oder auch in anderen Wohn- und Lebensbereichen: Das Airtec Picture setzt edle Akzente und gibt neuen Ideen Raum. Dabei beeindruckt nicht nur das Design – auch die Wirkungsweise ist einzigartig: Durch eine spezielle Keratinleinwand absorbiert das Bild Schadstoffe aus der Raumluft und wandelt diese in chemisch völlig ungiftige Substanzen um. Das Purelaine Airtec Picture arbeitet dabei nicht wie ein Filter, sondern wie ein biologischer Katalysator, der allein durch die Zirkulation der Raumluft, Schad- und Geruchsstoffe wie Formaldehyd, Ozon, Schwefeloxid und Stickstoffoxid neutralisiert.

Data and Facts		soda
Material | Material		natural wood, metal | Naturholz, Metall
Sustainability | Nachhaltigkeit		wood originating from sustainable forestry | Holz aus nachhaltiger Forstwirtschaft
Manufacture | Verarbeitung		natural oils and waxes | Natürliche Öle und Wachse
Design | Design		every pieces is unique | Jedes Stück ein Unikat

soda | ZEITRAUM

www.zeitraum-moebel.de

The furniture of ZEITRAUM appeals to people who appreciate what wood really is: a cultural asset—and therewith one of the oldest and most attractive materials. This is why ZEITRAUM exclusively uses healthy woods that are processed exactly as is appropriate according to their characteristics. The timber for each piece is individually selected and combined making it unique in terms of color and grain. Theses demanding pieces of furniture are exclusively made of wood originating from sustainable forestry. The table collection, designed by the design team Formstelle is therefore produced in beech, oak, wild oak, maple, American cherry as well as American and European nut. Due to the matt or glossy chromed and respectively brown-grey lacquered wire bow frame the topped off solid wood tabletop gains a certain easiness that is evocative of the handy foldable kitchen furniture of the 60s. Combined with chairs like Form or Calu, suites arise which convey the fine elegance, fancy high-quality and innovative retro-perspective.

Die Möbel von ZEITRAUM wenden sich an die Menschen, die schätzen was Holz ist: ein Kulturgut. Und damit einer der ältesten und reizvollsten Werkstoffe. ZEITRAUM verwendet deshalb nur gesunde Hölzer, die unter genauer Kenntnis ihrer Eigenschaften materialgerecht verarbeitet werden. Das Holz wird für jedes Möbel individuell ausgewählt und zusammengestellt – jedes Stück ist also einmalig in Farbe und Maserung. Zur Fertigung der anspruchsvollen Designermöbel werden ausschließlich Hölzer aus nachhaltiger Forstwirtschaft verwendet. Die Tischserie Soda, die von dem Designteam Formstelle entworfen wurde, wird deshalb in Buche, Eiche, Eiche wild, Ahorn, amerikanischer Kirsche sowie amerikanischem und europäischem Nussbaum gefertigt. Die abgerundete Massivholztischplatte erhält durch das matt oder glänzend verchromte bzw. braungrau lackierte Drahtbügelgestell eine Leichtigkeit, die an praktische Klapp-Küchenmöbel aus den 60er Jahren erinnert. Kombiniert mit Stühlen wie Form oder Calu ergeben sich so Sitzgruppen, die feine Eleganz, edle Hochwertigkeit und zugleich eine innovative Retro-Perspektive transportieren.

Data and Facts	Slab, Blow + Beat
Material	Material	local woods (Slab)	heimische Hölzer (Slab)
Manufacture	Verarbeitung	natural oak wood, oiled or stained (Slab)	natürliches Eichenholz, geölt oder gebeizt (Slab)
Technology	Technologie	designed for energy-saving lamps (Blow)	ausgelegt auf Energiesparlampen (Blow)

Slab, Blow + Beat | Tom Dixon

www.tomdixon.net

For the table and chair collection Slab, Tom Dixon focuses on natural oak wood which is naturally oiled or black stained. Tom Dixon purposefully processes local woods instead of naturally dark tropic wood. Inspired by the design of the popular tea table from the 50s, Slab's tabletop is topped off at the corners and the legs are slantly attached, giving the table a certain retro look. The stackable chair Slab is the matching further development of traditional, classy coffee house chairs, whose drawn forward back serves as a comfortable armrest at the same time. The slant legs of this chair perfectly match the table Slab. And the energy-saving lamp Blow provides for cozy and at the same time cool lighting above the suite. This copper-colored, golden glossy pendant light provides gentle light out of a glassy hemisphere. Exclusively low-energy compact fluorescent light bulbs can be used for this cool and elegant design lamp.

Bei der Tisch- und Stuhlserie Slab setzt Tom Dixon auf natürliches Eichenholz, das naturbelassen geölt oder auch schwarz gebeizt wird. So werden gezielt heimische Hölzer verarbeitet, anstatt natürlich dunkler Tropenhölzer. Inspiriert von der Form der beliebten 50er Jahre Teetische, ist die Tischplatte von Slab an den Ecken abgerundet und die Tischbeine sind im Retro-Look schräg angesetzt. Der stapelbare Stuhl Slab stellt die dazu passende Weiterentwicklung traditioneller, klassischer Kaffeehausstühle dar, deren nach vorne gezogene Lehne zugleich eine bequeme Ablagefläche für die Arme bietet. Die schräggestellten Beine des Stuhls harmonieren perfekt mit dem Tisch Slab. Und für gemütliches und gleichzeitig cooles Licht über der Sitzgruppe sorgt die Energiesparleuchte Blow. Die kupferfarbene, goldig glänzende Pendelleuchte spendet aus einer gläsernen Halbkugel sanftes Licht. Eingesetzt werden können in das kühle und elegante Designerstück ausschließlich fluoreszierende Energiespar-Glühbirnen.

Data and Facts	Strata
Material | Material	recycling wood, FSC birch ply | Recycling-Holz, FSC Schichtsperrholz
Sustainability | Nachhaltigkeit	recycling wood, which can be recycled itself | Recycling-Holz, das selbst wieder recycelt werden kann
Social commitment | Soziales Engagement	Co-operation with GreenWorks | Kooperation mit GreenWorks

Strata | Ryan Frank

www.ryanfrank.net

The strata line by Ryan Frank is a range of furniture consisting of a chair, stool, coffee table and dining table. Apart from the extraordinary design, strata provides another surprise when it comes to the material from which the line is built: the seating furniture are made of recycled wood from old, broken, redundant office furniture combined with FSC birch ply. The recycling wood originates from GreenWorks, a non-profit organization in Great Britain, the London designer co-operates with for this sustainable furniture collection. With such exceptional ideas, Ryan Frank does not necessarily want to want to comply with any eco rules—he just sets great value on the sustainability of his products: with good design and close-to-nature materials. As a result, the permanent use of recycled and recyclable materials brings out interior lines that are just as functional as unique, air ecological consciousness and, at the same time, are always also evidence of the eagerness to experiment and a certain sense of humor.

Die strata Serie von Ryan Frank besteht aus einem Lehnstuhl, einem Hocker, einem Kaffeetisch sowie einem Esstisch. Neben der außergewöhnlichen Formgebung bietet strata eine weitere Überraschung bei dem Material, aus dem die Serie angefertigt wird: die Sitzmöbel werden aus recyceltem Holz von alten, kaputten Büromöbeln, kombiniert mit FSC Schichtsperrholz aus natürlicher Birke hergestellt. Das Recyclingholz kommt von GreenWorks, einer karitativen Einrichtung in Großbritannien, mit der der Londoner Designer für diese nachhaltige Möbelserie kooperiert. Mit solch außergewöhnlichen Ideen möchte Ryan Frank sich keinen Öko-Regeln unterwerfen – er legt einfach nur Wert auf die Nachhaltigkeit seiner Produkte: durch gutes Design und naturnahe Materialien. So führt der ständige Einsatz von wiederverwerteten und recyclingfähigen Materialien zu Interieurserien, die ebenso funktional wie einzigartig sind. Dabei ökologisches Bewusstsein ausstrahlen und gleichzeitig immer auch von Experimentierfreudigkeit und einem gewissen Sinn für Humor zeugen.

Data and Facts		Natural wooden floors
Material	Material	FSC-certified wood from the US | FSC zertifiziertes Holz aus den USA
Sustainability	Nachhaltigkeit	reforestation of tree populations | Wiederaufforstung der Baumbestände
Design	Design	innovative plank floors | Innovative Dielenböden

Natural wooden floors | Ebony and Co

www.ebonyandco.com

Ebony and Co already exists since the early 60s. Back then, a small family business set about restoring old mansions with traditional plank floors. In the course of the years, Ebony and Co evolved into a path-breaking producer of wood floors who is open for innovations and sets design standards and always brings up the proper respect for nature. Thus, all woods Ebony and Co uses exclusively originate from sustainable cultivated forest areas of the American Northwest, which are most small and privately owned. The processed wood is accordingly very old and naturally grown without any fertilizers and pesticides. The wood is predominantly used for exceptionally long and wide plank floors which provide for a natural sense of space with a high demand to design—and some celebrity design lovers already recognized it. Therefore, Bill Clinton, Donna Karan and the Rockefeller family are, amongst others, renowned customers of Ebony and Co.

Das Unternehmen Ebony and Co existiert bereits seit den frühen 60er Jahren. Damals machte sich ein kleiner Familienbetrieb daran, alte Herrenhäuser mit traditionellen Dielenböden zu restaurieren. Im Laufe der Jahre entwickelte sich Ebony and Co zu einem wegweisenden Holzboden-Produzenten, der offen für Innovationen ist und Designmaßstäbe setzt. Und bei allem Tun eine gehörige Portion Respekt vor der Natur aufbringt. So stammen alle Hölzer, die Ebony and Co verwendet, ausschließlich von nachhaltig bewirtschafteten Forstflächen des amerikanischen Nordwestens, die meist klein und in privater Hand sind. Das verwendete Holz zeugt dementsprechend von hohem Alter und natürlichem Wachstum ohne Dünger und Pestizide. Eingesetzt wird es vorwiegend in Form außergewöhnlich langer und breiter Dielen. Diese sorgen für ein natürliches Raumgefühl mit hohem Designanspruch – was auch prominente Designliebhaber bereits erkannt haben. So zählen unter anderem Bill Clinton, Donna Karan und die Rockefeller Familie zum namhaften Klientel von Ebony and Co.

magnum, stretto, lux, eviva, cubus | TEAM 7

www.team7.at

The Austrian design and furnishing brand TEAM 7 creates natural furniture which are surprising with fancy shapes and puristic simplicity. Inspired by nature, the individual chairs, tables and benches are made of hardwood exclusively originating from sustainable forestry. All pieces of furniture are supplemented by recyclable glass and metal parts as well as precious, environmentally compatible textile or leather upholstery. Thus, predominantly wood is used for the table of the magnum line which has been awarded with the red dot award, whereas the backrests can be chosen to be the only elements made of wood in case of the filigree cantilever chairs. It is similar for the stretto line—however, contrasts are set here in case of the table by massive stainless steel feet and transparent glass leaves. The lux line provides for bright spots in the dining area thanks to light chairs leaving room between backrest and seat. The table of this line appears just as solid as straight and is really handy at the same time thanks to the fact that it can be extended. The new lux chair skillfully sets a pretty new priority here: it does entirely without wood and convinces with an airy design and gentle verves.

Die österreichische Design- und Einrichtungsmarke TEAM 7 schafft Naturmöbel, die mit extravaganten Formen und puristischer Schlichtheit überraschen. Inspiriert von der Natur, werden die individuellen Stühle, Tische und Bänke aus Laubholz gefertigt, das ausschließlich aus nachhaltiger Forstwirtschaft stammt. Ergänzt durch recyclingfähige Glas- und Metallteile sowie edle, schadstofffreie Stoff- und Lederpolster. So wird bei der mit dem red dot award ausgezeichneten Serie magnum das Material Holz vorwiegend für den Tisch genutzt, während bei den filigranen Freischwingern lediglich die Lehnen aus Holz gewählt werden können. Ähnlich sieht es bei der Serie stretto aus – jedoch werden hier auch beim Tisch Kontraste gesetzt: durch massive Standfüße aus Edelstahl und transparente Glaseinlegeplatten. Die Serie lux sorgt für Lichtblicke im Essbereich. Mit hellen Stühlen, die zwischen Lehne und Sitzfläche Raum lassen. Und einem Tisch, der ebenso massiv wie geradlinig wirkt und gleichzeitig mit seiner funktionalen Ausziehtechnik richtig praktisch ist. Der neue Stuhl lux setzt da gekonnt einen ganz neuen Akzent: Er kommt ganz ohne Holz aus und überzeugt mit luftigem Design und sanften Schwüngen.

Data and Facts	octo 4240, secto 4200, victo 4250
Material | Material	local birch wood | heimisches Birkenholz
Technology | Technologie	designed for energy-saving lamps | auf Energiesparlampen ausgerichtet
Fair Trade | Fair Trade	made in Finland by local handicraft businesses | made in Finnland von ortsansässigen Handwerksbetrieben

octo 4240, secto 4200, victo 4250 | Secto Design
www.sectodesign.fi

On the one side, an ecologically correct lighting is tightly interlinked with the energy consumption of a light source. On the other hand, it is also the materials of the lamp that are important, however. This is why the Finnish company Secto Design produces fascinating lamps created by light and interior designer Seppo Koho. All lamps are made of local birch wood originating from forestries with the international PEFC certificate. The innovative lamps are exclusively produced in Finland by local cabinet-makers. They are manufacturing Secto Design's ground-breaking, wooden pendant, wall or table lights which provide luminosity to create an astonishing light and atmosphere: a gleaming cone of light leaves the opening of the shade at the top while a diffuse luminosity develops between the individual, gently shaped laminated birch slats. Secto design recommends the use of energy-saving bulbs in warm white, being the perfect light source for the exceptional design lamps. For pleasant lighting and a good conscience.

Eine ökologisch korrekte Beleuchtung hängt zum einen eng mit dem Energieverbrauch einer Lichtquelle zusammen. Zum anderen aber auch mit den Materialien der Lampe selbst. Unter der kreativen Federführung von Licht- und Interior-Designer Seppo Koho fertigt die finnische Manufaktur Secto Design deshalb faszinierende Leuchten aus heimischem Birkenholz, das aus Forstbetrieben mit der internationalen PEFC-Zertifizierung stammt. Die neuartigen Lampen werden ausschließlich in Finnland von dort ansässigen Handwerkern hergestellt. Sie produzieren die innovativen, hölzernen Pendel-, Wand oder Tischlampen der Marke Secto Design, die ein erstaunliches Licht erzeugen: Zur Schirmöffnung hin fällt das Licht als strahlender Kegel heraus. Während an den Seiten eine diffuse Helligkeit zwischen den einzelnen, sanft geformten Holzleisten entsteht. Als ideales Leuchtmittel für die außergewöhnlichen Designerstücke empfiehlt Secto Design Energiespar-Glühbirnen in einem warmen, weißen Farbton. Für wohltuendes Licht und ein gutes Gewissen.

Data and Facts	Tischmich
Material | Material	oiled birch ply, natural linoleum | geöltes Birkensperrholz, natürliches Linoleum
Sustainability | Nachhaltigkeit	durable processing, unobtrusive design | langlebige Verarbeitung, zurückhaltendes Design
Production | Produktion	ecologically oriented workshop | ökologisch ausgerichtete Werkstätte
Fair Trade | Fair Trade	made in Germany | made in Germany

Tischmich | Nils Holger Moormann

www.moormann.de

The exceptional and, at the same time, indescribable easy foldable table "Tischmich" carries its own legs. To set the table up, the legs are taken from the bottom side of the table like over-dimensional jigsaw pieces. Inserted in pairs, the legs penetrate the surface of the table in a V-shape which makes the table stable and gives it its unmistakable appearance. This handy table with its unique arrow pattern in the tabletop has been designed by Jakob Gebert and produced in Nils Holger Moormann's designer workshop since then. Only two materials are used for the production of Tischmich: oiled birch ply and colored linoleum, which is made of natural materials such as jute fabric and linseed oil. The use of linoleum for the top of the table is just as unusual as perfect—for linoleum being heat-resistant and having a long-life fungicide and bacterio-static effect, after all, which makes it particularly hygienic.

Der außergewöhnliche und gleichzeitig unbeschreiblich einfache Klapptisch Tischmich trägt seine Beine in sich. Zum Aufbau werden sie wie überdimensionale Puzzleteile aus der Unterseite der Tischplatte gelöst. Paarweise zusammengesteckt, durchdringen die Beine V-förmig die Oberfläche und verleihen dem Tisch so Standfestigkeit und sein unverwechselbares Aussehen. Der praktische Tisch mit seinem einzigartigen Pfeilmuster in der Tischplatte wurde von Jakob Gebert entworfen und seitdem in der Designerwerkstätte von Nils Holger Moormann produziert. Bei der Herstellung von Tischmich kommen nur zwei Materialien zum Einsatz: geöltes Sperrholz aus natürlichem Birkenholz und farbiges Linoleum, das aus natürlichen Materialien wie Jutegewebe und Leinöl produziert wird. Die Linoleumplatte ist für den Einsatz am Esstisch ein ebenso ungewöhnliches wie ideales Material – ist Linoleum doch hitzebeständig und verfügt zudem über eine lebenslange fungizide und bakteriostatische Wirkung, was es besonders hygienisch macht.

Data and Facts		Sit	
Material | Material		natural wood, metal | Naturholz, Metall	
Sustainability | Nachhaltigkeit		wood from sustainable forestry | Holz aus nachhaltiger Forstwirtschaft	
Manufacture | Verarbeitung		natural oils and waxes | Natürliche Öle und Wachse	
Design | Design		every piece is unique | Jedes Stück ein Unikat	

Sit | ZEITRAUM

www.zeitraum-moebel.de

Surfaces play an important role in the furniture of ZEITRAUM. They feel smooth and smell fresh and natural. The latter comes from noble woods originating from sustainable forestry and the high-quality oils and waxes that are repeatedly massaged into the finely sanded surfaces, leaving the open pores of the wood free to breathe, to absorb and to give off moisture, whilst at the same time affording them the best of protection. The chairs and benches Sit developed by the designer Catharina Lorenz, who is working in Milan, are moreover made of oak, American cherry or American nut. The swinging, harmoniously proportioned chairs can be ordered, according to one's individual taste, with a fabric or leather upholstering or also plain without upholstery. Combined with the Sit bench and a ZEITRAUM table such as Pjur or Cena, individually arranged suites with a high-quality charisma and bubbly design.

Bei den Möbeln von ZEITRAUM spielen Oberflächen eine wichtige Rolle. Sie fühlen sich angenehm an und verbreiten einen frischen, natürlichen Duft. Dieser stammt von den edlen Hölzern aus nachhaltiger Forstwirtschaft sowie von den hochwertigen Ölen und Wachsen, die mehrmals in die fein geschliffenen Oberflächen einmassiert werden. Durch diese Behandlung kann die naturbelassene, offenporige Holzoberfläche atmen und ist gleichzeitig bestmöglich geschützt. Die von der in Mailand ansässigen Designerin Catharina Lorenz entworfenen Stühle und Bänke Sit werden dazu aus Eiche, amerikanischer Kirsche oder amerikanischem Nussbaum angefertigt. Die schwungvollen, harmonisch proportionierten Stühle können, ganz nach individuellem Geschmack, mit einer Stoff- oder Lederbepolsterung oder auch pur ohne Polster geordert werden. Zusammen mit der Sit Bank und einem ZEITRAUM Tisch, wie den Modellen Pjur oder Cena, ergeben sich individuell arrangierte Sitzgruppen mit einer hochwertigen Ausstrahlung und temperamentvollem Design.

Data and Facts		Interieur & Accessoires
Material	Material	natural wood, stainless steel, glass | Naturholz, Edelstahl, Glas
Sustainability	Nachhaltigkeit	wood originating from cut city trees | Verwendung von Holz gefällter Stadtbäume
Design	Design	puristic-rustic, each piece is unique | Puristisch-rustikal, jedes Stück ein Unikat

Interieur & Accessoires | sawadee design

www.sawadeedesign.de

Every object of sawadee design is made from Berlin city trees. Centuries of history can be found in the wooden structure of these Berlin originals. Some of the trees used were already planted in times of Frederick the Great and picture Berlin's history. There are, for instance, partially shell splinters or barbwire from the 2nd World War in the wood. Climatic conditions can also be retraced by means of the annual rings. Sawadee does not agglutinate or assemble, but works the objects out of massive logs in perfection. All objects are thoroughly dried, fine sanded and stand out for an extremely plain surface. The rustic and inimitable solid pieces of furniture, bowls and lamps are only partially supplemented by high-quality, recyclable materials such as stainless steel or glass. This is how sawadee design lets the ecologically correct liaison of nature and metropolis, of past and present become part of private living space.

Jedes Objekt von sawadee design wird aus dem Holz von gefällten Berliner Stadtbäumen gefertigt. Jahrhundertalte Geschichte findet sich in der hölzernen Struktur dieser Berliner Originale. Einige der verwendeten Bäume wurden bereits zur Zeit von Friedrich dem Großen gepflanzt und bilden Berliner Geschichte ab. So finden sich teilweise Granatsplitter oder auch Stacheldraht aus dem 2. Weltkrieg im Holz. Auch klimatische Gegebenheiten lassen sich anhand der Jahresringe nachvollziehen. Bei sawadee design wird nichts zusammengefügt oder geleimt, sondern in Perfektion aus massiven Stämmen herausgearbeitet. Alle Objekte werden sorgfältig getrocknet, fein geschliffen und zeichnen sich durch eine extrem glatte Oberfläche aus. Ergänzt werden die rustikalen und unnachahmlich massiven Möbelstücke, Schalen und Leuchten lediglich teilweise durch hochwertige, recyclingfähige Materialien wie Edelstahl oder Glas. So lässt sawadee design das ökologisch korrekte Zusammentreffen von Natur und Metropole, von Geschichte und Gegenwart Teil des privaten Wohnraums werden.

index

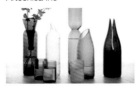

index

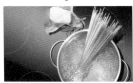

index

index

imprint

Bibliographic information published by the Deutsche Nationalbibliothek
The Deutsche Nationalbibliothek lists this publication in the Deutsche Nationalbibliografie; detailed bibliographic data are available in the Internet at http://dnb.d-nb.de.

ISBN: 978-3-89986-104-4

© 2008 avedition GmbH, Ludwigsburg
© 2008 Edited and produced by
fusion publishing GmbH, Stuttgart . Los Angeles

Printed in Austria
by Vorarlberger Verlagsanstalt AG, Dornbirn

Paper: EuroBulk by M-real Hallein AG
It is PEFC, DIN EN ISO 9001, DIN EN ISO 14001 and EMAS certified.

avedition GmbH
Königsallee 57 | 71638 Ludwigsburg | Germany
p +49-7141-1477391 | f +49-7141-1477399
www.avedition.com | contact@avedition.com

Team: Bianca Maria Öller (Author),
Katharina Feuer (Editorial management, Layout)
Jan Hausberg (Imaging & prepress),
Connexus GmbH, Sprachentransfer, Berlin (Translations)

Photocredits (product): courtesy Artecnicainc (TranSglass); courtesy Boris Bally (Bin There!, Flat Truss); courtesy bambu (Lacquerware, Nesting Baskets); courtesy Braun/ Procter&Gamble (Somelier Range); courtesy Bündnis für Glasdekogewebe (Glass deco fabrics); courtesy Christine Misiak (Recycling Teasets); courtesy Dedon (Spa, Soho); courtesy diefabrik (table 433, chair 777, shelf 114); courtesy Tom Dixon (EcoWare, Slab, Blow, backcover top left); courtesy Diy Kyoto (Wattson); courtesy Draper's Organic (Hemp Linen), courtesy Ebony and Co (Natural wooden floors); courtesy eco art studio (purelaine airtec picture); courtesy ekobo (Mikoto, Medio, Gemo); courtesy AEG/Electrolux (Ecological kitchen series); courtesy Fairfix (sit down, sit & eat); courtesy Stephen Lenthall & Ryan Frank (Strata); courtesy Grüne Erde (Enamel Pots, Jovanella); courtesy Hansen Living (Instant Kitchen, cover); courtesy husque (Bowls); courtesy Inter IKEA Systems B.V. (Kitchen system Faktum); courtesy Matthieu Lehanneur (O, Local River, Bel Air); courtesy Liebherr Hausgeräte GmbH (Cooling units); courtesy mixko (Coron, Delight, Kimono); courtesy Nils Holger Moormann GmbH/Jäger & Jäger (Erika, Tischmich, backcover top right); courtesy Nespresso (Le Cube & Latissima); courtesy Presso (Presso Coffee Maker); courtesy rice (Mixed Tableware, backcover bottom right); courtesy Sawadee (Interieur & Accessoires); courtesy Schock (LED Sink); courtesy Secto Design (octo 4240, secto 4200, victo 4250, backcover bottom left); courtesy sidebyside-design (Tray Up, Dishtowel Loop); courtesy Siemens (KG29WE60); courtesy Simplehuman (Recycler); courtesy Team 7 (k7, linee, magnum, stretto, lux, eviva, cubus); courtesy Rosenthal (Free Spirit); courtesy Zeitraum (soda, sit); courtesy Schott Zwiesel (Serving & More, Wine & Bar)

Bianca Maria Öller
The author and copywriter lives and works in Munich. She finds inspiration in both innovative design and outside in nature.

Bianca Maria Öller
Die Autorin und Texterin lebt und arbeitet in München. Inspiration findet sie in innovativem Design ebenso wie draußen in der Natur.

green designed series:

green designed: Future Cars
green designed: Fashion

Further information and links at
www.bestdesigned.com
www.fusion-publishing.com

All books are released in German and English